W9-BRH-742

"By turns honest and heartbreaking, Larson's book is a celebration of inner strength. It is also a poignant reminder that the mark of a true warrior is not just someone who fights wars but who also knows how to also 'ask for help' in times of crisis. A courageous and inspiring memoir."

—*Kirkus Reviews*

"*Warrior* is a vivid and intensely personal a ccount of Dr. Theresa Larson's extraordinary life as caregiver, high-level athlete, combat veteran, and bulimia survivor. The book is powerful, inspirational, and underscores how we can all be both strong and vulnerable at the same time. Theresa opens her heart and soul on every page and we closed the book feeling uplifted by her amazing spirit."

—Kelly and Juliet Starrett, CEOs of MobilityWOD and
 San Francisco CrossFit and cofounders of StandUPKids.org

"I have always believed that being vulnerable does not imply weakness, but rather the courage to be authentic, to live as who you are, not as the person others expect you to be. Theresa Larson walks us through her journey to get to authenticity. She shows us what it means to be a warrior and anyone will identify with her struggles and learn from her, learn that they too can be resilient, healthy and a true warrior. Bravo Theresa Larson. A must-read!"

—Eva Selhub, M.D., author of *Your Health Destiny*, stress and
 mind-body medicine specialist, and former instructor in
 medicine at Harvard Medical School and associate in medicine
 at the Massachusetts General Hospital

"Marines are tough. Marines are hard core. Marines cannot fail. *Warrior* reveals the struggles that come along with this desire for perfection. Theresa shows that real strength happens when you summon the courage to conquer these addictive and doomed expectations. Theresa's willingness to share her journey makes her a true hero and one of the bravest Marines I know."

—Mike Burgener, former Marine, Senior International Weightlifting Coach for the United States, Head Strength Coach for CrossFit

"Raw. Real. Rousing. *Warrior* will challenge your beliefs about real strength. Theresa Larson has crafted a memoir that will leave readers finding parallels to their own lives. From the pain of losing a loved one to struggles with food and self-esteem, Larson dives deep and looks back to get at the 'why.' *Warrior* is a story of hope and transformation, of calling on the strength that already lives inside. You'll put it down and ask, 'What's possible for me?' It's that good."

—Steph Gaudreau, bestselling author of *The Performance Paleo Cookbook* and *The Paleo Athlete*

"Theresa Larson's memoir reveals the complex self-savagery of surviving bulimia in a war zone. The conflict may have looked like Iraq on the outside, but the real enemy was her own mind. This book is a rare glimpse into the secret world of a bulimic and exposes the multiple traumas that coalesced into this disease as a means of coping. As a former bulimic, I was at once repulsed, enthralled, and redeemed by Theresa's willingness to be so vulnerable on every page. A must-read for those in mental health, armed services, and health and fitness fields."

—Jill Miller, author of *The Roll Model: A Step by Step Guide to Erase Pain, Improve Mobility and Live Better in Your Body*

"As a Marine officer, I feel sad at the collective failure in our responsibility to take care of and be faithful to one of our own. So many times, we have said and heard 'Suck it up, Marine.' This story reminds me to look through strength and beauty, realize a person's struggles, and dedicate time to take care of them."

—Alyce Fernebok, former Marine Captain

WARRIOR

A Memoir

THERESA LARSON

& ALAN EISENSTOCK

HarperOne
An Imprint of HarperCollinsPublishers

HarperOne

I have changed the names of some institutions and individuals, and modified identifying features, including physical descriptions, locations and occupations, in order to preserve the anonymity of the individuals and the institutions. In some cases, composite characters have been created or timelines have been compressed, in order to further preserve privacy and to maintain narrative flow. The goal in all cases was to protect people's privacy without damaging the integrity of the story.

HarperCollins books may be purchased for educational, business, or sales promotional use. For information please e-mail the Special Markets Department at SPsales@harpercollins.com.

HarperCollins website: http://www.harpercollins.com

FIRST EDITION

Designed by Janet M. Evans

Library of Congress Cataloging-in-Publication Data
Larson, Theresa, author.
 Warrior : a memoir / Theresa Larson & Alan Eisenstock.)—1st edition.
    pages cm
  ISBN 978-0-06-239948-9 (hardcover)—ISBN 978-0-06-239950-2
(e-book) 1. Larson, Theresa, author. 2. Iraq War, 2003-2011)—Personal
narratives, American. 3. Women marines)—Biography. 4. United States.
Marine Corps)—Military life. 5. Bulimia)—Patients)—Biography. 6.
Women athletes)—United States)—Biography. I. Eisenstock, Alan, author.
II. Title.
 DS79.766.L37A3 2016
 956.7044'345092)—dc23
 [B]
                                                        2015033615

---

16 17 18 19 20   RRD(H)   10 9 8 7 6 5 4 3 2 1

To the most legit and amazing man in my life, my adventure buddy, my best friend: Per Larson, who is my Bucket List of a husband.

To my big brothers Paul and Bob, for being my role models!

*"It takes the courage and strength
of a warrior to ask for help."*

—DAVID FINKEL,
Thank You for Your Service

CONTENTS

THE LAST CONVOY

I SIT ON THE FLOOR OF MY ROOM, MY BACK CREASED into the wall. My mouth feels dry, my lips cracked. I sniff and wipe my nose with the back of my hand.

I pick the envelope off the floor and stare at it. I start to open it, and my hand shakes. Finally I direct my quivering fingers—long and scarred, my nails nubs, the skin as brown and hard as the desert outside—toward the envelope's sealed flap. I open the envelope carefully, almost daintily, somehow without tearing the paper. I ease the letter out. I read the first two words and choke back a sob.

"Dearest Theresa."

With my thumb I smother a tear that snakes down my cheek and keep reading.

"Dad is sitting here at his desk with an overwhelming pride for you, as well as deep concern, almost worry. I'm proud that you are who you are—God's child, my child—who is doing her very best every day of her life. While you affect so many people with your stature and attitude, your life is on a merry-go-round. If you want to stay mentally healthy, then get off and seek help now."

I feel myself go cold. My entire body shivers. I bring my legs tight into my chest. The letter flutters in my trembling hands.

"The key ingredient is your willingness to get help. If it is put off, it will be a silent cancer that will kill you."

I'm crying full force now, tears raining down my face, splashing onto the bottom lip of the letter. My chest heaves.

"You're a very special miracle, who has done more in twenty-four and a half years than most people will do in their dreams. . . . The irony of your situation is that you are in a war, your enemy is not from without but from within. . . . You are a very courageous person, Theresa, for facing your problems straight on. You cannot hope to take care of others properly if you cannot take care of yourself. . . ."

I exhale slowly, trying to halt my hands from shaking, my heart from galloping, my head from spinning. I fasten my eyes on the last sentence of the letter.

"I know that you will do what is right, Theresa. I love you, Dad."

My hands trembling, I fold the letter and slide it back into the envelope.

"I will, Dad," I say. "I will."

I see the mental health officer, a Navy psychologist. I sit in his stark waiting area across from a heavyset, older nurse who overwhelms a small metal desk as she loudly files papers. I jump every time I hear a noise—the whap of the nurse closing a file folder, a phone ringing, laughter from outside the hut. I don't want any of my Marines to see me in here. I feel nervous and unsteady. And I feel ashamed. Once or twice I notice the nurse looking at me. I can't read her eyes. I'm not sure if she's judging me or somehow sharing my pain, understanding my fear. I check my watch. I've been waiting fifteen minutes.

I can't do this. I can't wait for this guy any longer. I stand, turning to leave, and his office door opens. A man in his late thirties, short, nearly bald, a few greasy strands of hair lying tortured across his scalp like a newly tarred three-lane highway, stands in the doorway. He tries a smile, going for sympathy or warmth, I can't tell, but either way the smile doesn't work, and then he ushers me into his office like a game show host. I walk past him— I tower over him—and catch a last glance from the nurse.

In his office, the Navy shrink does the same game-show gesture toward a chair across from his desk. I sit down heavily. I feel as if I'm in high school, summoned before the principal.

The guy waits, folds his hands beneath his chin, and after another of those confusing smiles, says in a surprisingly deep voice, "So, Lieutenant Hornick, how can I help?"

I shift in the chair, buying time. I look past him, and I say, low, "I'm struggling, sir." I swallow a gob of something sour that has suddenly risen into my throat. I paw the floor with my boot and speak again in a soft, distant voice, so distant it feels as if another person, not me, has spoken from another room. "I have . . . I *may* have . . . possibly . . . an eating disorder."

"Oh?"

"Bulimia," I add, quickly.

"Okay." He lowers his hands flat on his desk. "What are your symptoms?"

3

I want to flee. Or shove this guy against the wall.

"I throw up," I say, throttling a burning ripple of impatience. "I can't control what I eat." My mouth feels dry, and the room slowly starts to whirl. I wrap my arms around my stomach. "I throw up," I say again, urgently, as if I might heave right here. "I'm not sure what to do. I need . . . help."

"Uh-huh," the shrink says. He flicks his fingers like he's playing an imaginary keyboard on his desk. "What are you dealing with? What are your stressors?"

I tighten my arms around my middle. I suddenly feel a fireball of rage scorching my insides. I force myself to speak in a near whisper; otherwise I know I will scream. "I'm an *officer*," I say.

"Yes."

"I'm in charge of . . . so many people . . . in my command. I run convoys several times a week. I'm an insurgent escort for the regimental commander."

The lines in his forehead undulate like waves.

"I escort female insurgents," I say, hoping that with this clarification he will comprehend what I'm saying. "I'm under a lot of pressure. A lot of stress. Stressors? You want a list? We're in a war zone."

"Yes, I see. That is a lot of stress for a woman Marine."

I burn a stare into him. "I prefer to be called just a Marine, sir."

He flushes. "Of course, yes. I think, then, that we have to figure out how to manage your . . . *behavior* . . . with your stressors. . . ."

I don't hear much else. My arms flop to my sides. I sit on my hands and try to latch onto the words I see floating out of his mouth trapped in air bubbles, random words, connected in no way to the word preceding or following—" . . . *journal . . . triggers . . .*

another session . . ."—and then, on wobbly legs, I somehow find myself outside the Navy shrink's closed door, gripping the edge of the nurse's desk for balance.

"Do you want a glass of water?"

I nod.

I hear the scraping of a chair. The swish and rustle of movement. Water trickling into a glass from a pitcher. The nurse presses a cool glass into my hand. I gulp down the water. Thoughts swirl. *Get the fuck out of here. Cry. Lead my Marines. Throw up.*

"You shouldn't say anything." The nurse stands a foot away from me. She gently rests her hand on my shoulder. "You can't."

"I'm not sure I—"

"These walls are thin. I know what you're dealing with." She pauses, perhaps gathering up her own courage or deciding how much she should reveal to me, a stranger, technically her superior. "I've had bulimia for twenty years."

I look at the closed door, then back at the nurse.

"If you admit this to your company or your battalion, you'll be done," the nurse says. "You'll lose your career. You'll never get it back. I can't afford that. I'm divorced, got two small kids."

I again look at the shrink's door.

"He's all right. He knows about me. He just doesn't get it." She speaks rapidly through a funnel of pursed lips. "You have to be careful who you tell. Be very careful who you talk to."

She takes the empty glass from my hand, places it on her desk, sits, and dives back into her paperwork. I feel that for one moment she lowered a partition between us, and now she has brought it back up with a thud. I absently rub a file on her desk. "So, how do you—?"

"You suck it up," the nurse says, hard and far away. "You deal."

I head back to my room, my head throbbing, my stomach in a clinch. Before I reach my barracks, I take a detour and go directly to my safe place: the bathroom. I flip the sign on the door to "*Women*," go to the sink, and start scrubbing my hands. I look at myself in the mirror, and I think, *I have work to do.* In a matter of days, the free people of Iraq will elect their first permanent National Assembly under the new constitution. It's our job to oversee the elections, to make sure they're conducted properly, the voters protected, safe. I will lead a convoy of thirty or more trucks, 150 Marines. We will set up jersey barriers—barricades—to control the flow of traffic at the polls. I have come this far, fought this hard, and now I have a ton of work to do, planning, organizing, scheduling, training . . .

You can do this, Theresa, I say to my smudged reflection. *You can do it. Once more. One last time.*

I move away from the mirror and get down on my knees. I look toward the heavens.

"Help me," I whisper.

Deal, I think.

I lift the toilet lid, stick my finger down my throat, and for the fourth time today, I throw up.

2

IN DREAMS SHE CAME

1981–1991 / WOODWAY, WASHINGTON

I AM SIX YEARS OLD. WHIPPET-THIN, HEAD COCKED, dirty blond hair flying, a hot-wired bolt of energy packed inside my brother's faded flannel shirt, which brushes my scabby knees. I cannot sit still. Even when the family goes to church on Sunday and I'm wearing my pretty calico dress Mom made herself, even when we're sitting in the front row so we can hear Mom sing in the choir, trying to pick out her voice among the others, I feel as if my body is pulsing, poised to blast off like a rocket. I've always been this way. Born to *move*. Desperate to keep up with my crazy older brothers, racing, running, grappling, biking, always on the move themselves.

Our family, the Hornicks—my mom, Mary Ann, my dad, Joseph, my brothers, Bob and Paul, and me—live in a log cabin on over an acre of land in Woodway, a tiny town outside Seattle made up of houses with big backyards abutting a forest. My dad built the log cabin himself, with a little help from some friends, on weekends and days off from his commodity broker job. The log cabin is one huge room, wide and bright, the sun pouring in from glass ceilings and skylights. In the front as you walk in, past a braided blue-and-white rug, sit three small tree stumps where we put our shoes—the tallest stump for Bob, the middle one for Paul, the smallest for me. Looking back, I find it funny that the three of us were ever identified by "stumps," me being the shortest among us at six one.

Bookshelves, a grand piano, cushy couches, and a wood-burning stove fill the wide-open living area downstairs. A spiral staircase winds upstairs to a loft, which eventually becomes my room. For now, though, because I'm the youngest and the only girl, my room is just off the main downstairs area. Life seems "normal," even uneventful, until one night, when everything changes.

Mom tells us the news at dinner.

"I'm sick," she says. For a moment I hear only a hush, and then my world seems to go dark.

"I'm getting treatment, going to the hospital, taking a very strong medicine. I have a very good doctor."

Nobody speaks for a while. Then my older brother Bob clears his throat. "What do you mean . . . sick? What do you have?"

My mom looks at my dad. I can see that they're holding hands under the table.

"Cancer," my mom says.

My brother Paul absently turns his plate in a slow circle. "Are you . . . ?"

"I'm going to be all right," Mom says. "I'm going to be fine."

I look at my family, take in their faces, my two older brothers, my dad, and then I look at my mom. She smiles at me. She smiles, but I can see through her smile, even though I just turned six. We're outnumbered in this family, three to two, and when Mom brushes my hair, she sometimes says, "We girls have to stick together."

We have a way of looking at each other and knowing what the other is thinking without saying a word. We just know. And tonight, the night she tells us the news, I know she's scared.

I go with her to chemotherapy. I sit on her bed in a curtained-off space the size of a closet before she's hooked up with needles in her arms to a bunch of liquids in plastic packets, then I pull a chair next to her bed and hold her hand. After a while, she falls asleep and I work on my coloring book. At home after her treatment, she spends most of her days in bed or in the bathroom throwing up. Soon her hair starts falling out. She buys a wig and a batch of colorful scarves. I go shopping with her, and together we pick out a fancy scarf that she says she'll save for special occasions. I don't say much when I'm with her, but when I'm alone, I pray. She doesn't have to tell me she's in terrible pain. I just look at her. We look at each other. And I know.

My father quits his job and starts a vending machine business out of our house. He wants to spend more time at home with my mother. He works nights doing deliveries, and sometimes I go with him. He tries to be optimistic, even upbeat, but I can see he's living in his own private sorrow. One night, during a delivery, I start to doze off on the way home, my head leaning against the glass of the window. Nearly asleep, I feel his hand gently touch my arm, and I hear him say to me, or to himself, or to a vision of my mother, or perhaps to God, "I'm doing the best I can."

My mother's a fighter. She tries to keep her spirits up and live a normal life, or as normal as she can. She goes to church, helps me with my homework, and some days drops me off and picks me up at school. On rare occasions, we even go shopping. One day, after a year or so, my father gathers us for an early dinner and announces that the cancer has gone into remission. My mother lowers her head and nods and cries. I blink back tears and whisper a prayer of thanks. But then, not long after, the cancer comes back.

This time we know it's the end. None of us talks about it that way, but I stop praying for the cancer to go away. I just pray for my mother to not be in pain.

I read to her almost every night, and one night, as I settle in with a book, she says, "Sing for me tonight, Theresa."

I laugh. "You're the singer, Mommy. I have a voice like a mule."

"You have a beautiful voice. Come on. Let me hear you sing."

She reaches out and squeezes my hand. Her fingers seem so light, and as pale as a ghost's.

"I don't know what to sing," I say, but then on her nightstand I see the CD from *Phantom of the Opera*, her favorite musical of all time. I don't really know the songs from the show, but she's played the CD so often that I'm able to croak the first line, "In sleep he sang to me . . . in dreams he came . . ."

She beams.

I keep going.

"That voice which calls to me and speaks my name . . ."

I stumble through the rest of the song, making up lyrics as I go, humming when I have to, and coming to the coda, my voice rises theatrically, holding and screeching the last line, "THE PHANTOM OF THE OPERAAA IS HERE!!!"

I bow. Mom squeals and applauds weakly but with all her heart.

Another time she doesn't want me to sing or read to her. She just wants to talk. She pats the bed next to her. I curl up and lie next to her, our heads touching on her pillow. "I want you to know something, Theresa."

"Okay, Mom," I say, feeling a sense of dread.

She holds until she knows I'm not only listening, I'm hearing. "I'm not going to get to see a lot of things," she says. "I'll miss your eighth-grade graduation. Your high school graduation. Your prom. Taking you to college . . ." She pauses and takes a deep breath. "But I will always be with you. Inside you. Always."

I bite my lip.

"You need to live your life, Theresa, *live* it. Believe in yourself. Believe in God. And always keep going forward. Don't look back. Keep moving."

"I will."

"I want you to know something else. The most important thing." She lifts her head off the pillow and slowly, painfully sits up. She looks at me, her stare a laser. "Don't be afraid. Things could get bad . . . things *do* get bad . . . but you can't let anything stop you. Ever."

"I won't. I promise."

She drops her head back onto the pillow. "Life's not fair, Theresa. But you can't dwell on that. You can't let that get you down. Life is *not* fair. But that's never the point."

>>>

I help Mom pack a go bag with her medication, some snacks for us, and several bottles of water. I watch as she meticulously winds her special-occasion scarf over her wig and help her tie a knot under her chin. We load up the car and prepare for a rare road trip. We are driving to Vancouver, British Columbia, two and a half hours away, to see a production of *Phantom of the Opera*. Bob and Paul promise to behave and not torture me or each other on the trip as long as I promise not to sing. My brothers and I shake on it.

I sit next to Mom during the play. She watches, riveted through the first act, her eyes filling with tears during the songs. After intermission, into the second act, she starts to get restless. She grunts a few times and shifts in her seat, attempting to get comfortable. At one point she snaps her eyes closed and grabs my father's hand. After the play, as we begin the short walk to the parking lot, my mom stops abruptly. She's in too much pain to continue. My brothers and I move her out of the way of the people flowing out of the theater and wait with her while my dad gets the car.

About an hour into the drive home, my mother starts to cry. She asks for her pain pills. Bob rummages through her bag and hands her the bottle, which has only two pills left. Mom gulps them down with a bottle of water I hand her and closes her eyes. Twenty minutes later, she starts to moan. The pain, dulled momentarily, returns with a fury and begins to overwhelm her. She tries to find a comfortable position in her seat, but moving around intensifies the pain. She moans again, louder, and then, always the gentle soul, always a lady, she apologizes. From the backseat, I see my dad grip the steering wheel, his knuckles turning white, his eyes slits zeroing in on the road. Less than a half hour from home, Bob says quietly, "We drove past our exit."

"We're going to the hospital," my dad says.

>>>

At home a week later, Dad moves Mom out of their bedroom into the living room, setting up her hospital bed under the skylight. Hospice care workers attend her regularly, and friends, family, and people from the church arrive every day to keep Mom company and clumsily say their good-byes. One woman from the church, the harp soloist, comes once a week, lugging her harp, which she sets up in a corner of the living room and strums soothingly for an hour. My mother dozes during most of these visits. When she wakes briefly, she gazes at her visitors through filmy, unresponsive eyes.

Dad sleeps on the living room couch next to Mom. I carry my sleeping bag out of my room every night and roll it out on the floor at her feet. I sit with her and do my homework or read to her, and sometimes, softly, I sing. When I feel myself starting to fade, I crawl inside my sleeping bag. One night, before I go to sleep, her breathing slower, more labored, I take her hand and say, "I don't want you to be alone." And then I lean in and whisper an even deeper truth, "I don't want to be alone."

After a couple of months, fewer people visit. Restless all day at school, I rush home as soon as the bell rings. Thinking only about my mother, I forget to do my homework. I fall behind in my classes, and my grades suffer. I want to spend every minute I can, every waking minute, with my mom. But sometimes I'm not sure if she even knows I'm here.

"Do you think she realizes I'm with her?" I ask my dad.

"Oh, she knows, Theresa. And being here with her, the time you're spending with her, that is love. Doesn't matter what you say to her—even if you say nothing—that is love. Time is love."

Every night before I get into my sleeping bag, I kiss her on the forehead, squeeze her hand, and tell her I love her. But I don't have to. She knows.

⟩⟩⟩

My mom passes away at four o'clock in the morning. I'm asleep. In a dream, I feel something pass over me, something floating, then I see my mom's face, smiling, and I wake up. My dad kneels next to me, shaking my shoulder. I blink myself awake.

"Mom passed," he says, tears streaming down his face. "I was with her. I held her hand. It was beautiful, Theresa. I could see her soul lifting. There was a light rising off her body."

She's free I say to myself. *She's not going to be in pain anymore.*

I bow my head.

God answered my prayer.

I have no idea that her loss will carve a permanent hole in my heart.

At her funeral, I wear a dress my mom made me and an enormous bow in my hair that we made together. My dad, my brothers, and I help carry the casket. At the service I read a passage from the Bible, I think. I'm not sure. Everything that day feels hazy and unreal. I feel as if I'm standing apart from everything, a bystander. It's like I'm watching a movie of somebody else's life.

>>>

I spend the next week walking through each day as if my feet are stuck in cement. I hear the words "I'm sorry" so many times I want to scream. A couple of weeks after my mother's funeral, my dad insists that my brothers and I go to grief counseling for children who have lost parents. We enter a stuffy room in a church basement and take seats in the back row as a kid my age shares a story about his mom's death. Squirming in my folding chair, I whisper to my brother Bob, "I don't want to hear this."

"We'll leave as soon as—"

"Bob, I can't *breathe*." I shoot out of my chair and sprint out the door. Outside, I lean over, rest my hands on my knees, and gulp breath after breath of air.

I raise my head and look up into the sky. "Mommy," I say.

It's all I can say.

I am ten years old.

3

MY FIRST PLATOON

GRADES 4–8 / SAINT LUKE'S SCHOOL

Afternoons and weekends, we play basketball, usually Dad and me against Bob and Paul. We play to win.

When Bob guards me, he goes easy. He keeps his elbows in, doesn't body me up in the lane, mostly shoots from the outside. He's seventeen, six feet eight, a star at Seattle Prep. He dominates every game he plays, including this one, the one outside our barn, the backboard nailed to a tree.

Paul, fifteen, *has* to win and goes all out. He'll elbow me, grab me, shove me, slap me. If I call a foul on him, he looks stunned, and as soon as Dad turns his back, he gives me the finger. Paul doesn't know that we share the same obsession: I need to win as much as he does.

Except the team I'm on never wins in these games, and it kills me. Paul and Bob are just too strong and too competitive. Paul, I think, resents me and believes that Dad favors me, not just in these backyard games but all the time. When Dad says, "Paul, don't be so rough on her, it's only a game," it doesn't help. It's not just a game, to any of us.

What my brothers don't know and what I will never tell them is that I look up to them. The truth is, I want to *be* them. Well, mirrors of them. I don't want to be a boy, but since Mom died, I don't much like being a girl. I'm not interested in wearing girly clothes or getting my hair or nails done, or going to the mall. Everyone knows this. At school, I'm not invited into the cool cliques—I'm not invited into *any* cliques—so I keep to myself. I've become an outcast with very few friends. I'm *that* girl, the one whose mom died. I'm different, bordering on weird. I'm taller than all the other girls—by a lot—quieter, more awkward socially, and mainly interested in sports.

Even if I did care about the way I looked and wanted a trendy wardrobe, Dad wouldn't be able to help me the way Mom would have. He feels that sort of thing is materialistic and shallow, not to mention that we're on a strict budget because money's always tight. He sees no problem with me mostly wearing my brothers' hand-me-downs. I go to Saint Luke's, a parochial school. We wear uniforms every day. That makes it easy. If I need to go somewhere after school or on the weekend, I just throw on one of Paul's old flannel shirts over my jeans. If I complain that I have no clothes of my own, my dad takes me shopping at Goodwill.

At school, during lunch or recess, I usually sit alone. Sometimes I stare at this one group of girls, several of whom used to be my friends, and wish they would include me. The thought rapidly dissolves, because I know that even if they did bring me in, I wouldn't know what to say. I've become closed, socially clumsy, and very shy. Worst of all, I feel like a reject, as if having lost my mom has somehow made me inferior, even damaged.

One day during lunch, I see a group of girls circling around someone I know only slightly, Alisha, a heavyset girl in my class. The girls are taunting her, calling her "Fat-ass" and "Loser," then they get more insulting and obscene. Alisha cowers and begins to cry. I push myself away from the lunch table, where I'm eating alone as usual, and shove my way through the circle to Alisha. I pull up next to her, stand between her and the other girls, ball my hands into fists, and feeling the heat rise to my cheeks, I pick out the leader of the pack and stick my face an inch from hers. "Leave her alone," I say. "She's a human being. Her name is Alisha."

I glare at this girl, daring her to say something to me, wishing she'd put a hand on me, willing her to do it. "Maybe you'd like to say something to me," I say. "Why don't you call me a name?"

The girl reddens, realizes that if she says one word, I will knock her the hell out. With two years of unchecked rage roiling inside, I wouldn't mind letting off a little steam. I shift my feet, waiting for her to make a move. She backs away, her friends following her in retreat.

"Come on, Alisha, let's go." I put an arm around her and escort her through the remnants of this so-called inner circle, slightly surprised at the courage I managed to dredge up, relishing that I'm a teeny bit of a badass.

Alisha and I don't become more than nodding acquaintances after that, but nobody picks on her again.

>>>

My dad practices a no-nonsense parenting style of equal parts discipline and tough love. He runs our family like a military unit, he the officer in charge and we kids the lowly recruits. He orders us to report on our schoolwork and assigns chores, all of us taking turns cleaning the house, hauling in wood from outside (my least favorite chore, especially in winter), feeding our small menagerie of pigs, sheep, chickens, cats, and dogs, and cooking dinner three nights a week. Bob, a budding chef, enjoys cooking and comes up with a variety of scrumptious and exotic entrees, such as Thai noodle pasta and chicken parmesan, having chopped off the chicken's head earlier that day (I take it back: *that's* my least favorite chore). I create my one signature dish, a delightful taco salad, about which Paul grumbles, "Taco salad again? Really?" When it's his turn, Paul, with all the enthusiasm of a hair-netted cafeteria worker, throws together half-hearted grilled cheese sandwiches, scorching the toast into charred, inedible shingles and filling the kitchen with smoke, about which I say, "Burning the house down again? Really?"

Of course, we have to eat everything on our plates to be excused and are not allowed to complain about the quality of the cooking. If a complaint slips out, Dad says, "You have two choices: take it or leave it."

We know if we leave the food that's served, we're not allowed to ask for anything else and have to go to bed without supper. The guys, Dad included, don't exactly have discriminating palates. They inhale every morsel on their plates. They eat fast and they eat a lot, often going back for seconds, even when Paul serves up his blackened grilled cheese tiles.

Dad pushes us to take up a sport. Bob, already a high school basketball legend at Seattle Prep, for the most part knows how to deal with Dad, keeping both his cool and his distance, rarely making waves. Paul, slammed in the middle between Bob, the prodigal son, and me—according to him, daddy's little girl—rebels by acting out, fighting with Bob, torturing me, and testing Dad. When he chooses a sport, he picks golf, a sport he grows to love, one Dad never gets. I choose two sports—cross-country, because I'm the strongest runner in my class, and basketball, because I'm tall, Bob plays, and Dad thinks I should.

It's not easy living among all men. I do my best to navigate my way around Paul's moods and Dad's demands. Sometimes I feel like I'm walking through a minefield. At one point I move out of my room and into the loft so I can have my own space and keep above the steadily rising tide of testosterone. I choose to spend much of my time in my room, alone, except when my brothers head outside to run, bike, hike, shoot hoops, or play catch. I want to be part of that. I want to compete with them because I want them to respect me. I'm as good as they are, and I want them to include me. In fact, I *need* them to include me, because the truth is I don't really have any friends.

Bob and Paul become Boy Scouts. This means that I too want to be a Boy Scout. I tell this to Dad. As Paul rolls his eyes, Dad suggests that I try Girl Scouts first.

I attend one Girl Scout meeting, the troop made up of a group of girls from my school that I avoid and who avoid me. We spend the meeting baking cookies, mending clothes, and reciting a bunch of lame pledges. I want to punch my fist through a wall. I tell Dad I refuse to go back and that I will never be a Girl Scout.

"Why not?" he asks. "Give me one good reason."

"Because it's for *girls*," I say.

Dad gives in. To my brothers' annoyance, I accompany them and my dad on a Boy Scout hike and campout. I don't need to get special permission from the troop leader. The troop leader is Dad.

During the hike, I keep pace with my brothers and the rest of the troop. As we cross the clearing back to the campsite, I hear someone say, "She can hike better than a lot of these guys," and then I hear Paul answer, "Yeah, well, we don't want her here."

Of course, I'm crushed, but I shake it off because I've proven myself to them, to Dad, and to myself.

>>>

I make the eighth-grade basketball team. No shock there, having put in countless hours playing backyard hoops against my brothers, especially Bob, who's one of the best players in the state. I'm built for the sport—I'm tall, strong, and fast—and I've developed an unstoppable hook shot. I'm a natural center, the next Hornick to become a hoop star.

There's only one problem. Every time our point guard passes me the ball, I freeze. I'm not sure why. At least not at first.

My dad tries to help in his own way, the only way he knows how. With him coaching me, pushing me, we put in extra hours after practice in the gym and work out at home in the backyard until it gets dark. I don't mind this. I never back down from a challenge, and I actually like working out with Dad. The extra work pays off. I improve in practice. But during games, I fall apart.

"What's the matter with you?" Dad says in the car on the way home after a typical game in which I looked and felt disinterested on the court. "I don't understand. You had so many opportunities to score. You have to get in there. You have to be aggressive."

"I'll try."

"That's a rubber word," he says. "Either you do something or you don't."

Lying in bed that night, staring at the ceiling, visualizing myself on the court, at a loss, as frozen as a statue, not wanting the ball, wanting to *hide*, it hits me. To play basketball well, you have to *react*. I don't want that. I want to play a sport where I'm in charge.

I want to be in control.

4

TALENT

T*hwack.*

"Ow!" My brother Bob leaps out of his crouch, flings his catcher's mitt to the side, and shakes his fingers frantically. "Son of a bitch." He glares at me standing forty feet away on the pitcher's mound we've made out of packed-down dirt and dried leaves in the backyard. "Where'd you learn to pitch?"

"I watched a girl in the park," I say.

"She on a team?"

"The Diamond Dusters. She's older. Fifteen."

"Let me catch her," Paul says. He's lying on his back, legs crossed at his ankles, a blade of grass poking through his teeth.

"Be my guest," Bob says, tossing him the catcher's mitt.

Paul slips the mitt on, crouches, flattens the palm of his throwing hand in the wedge of dirt we've outlined in chalk, home plate, then holds the mitt up, offering me a perfect target.

I bend over, straighten slowly, whirl my arm into a slingshot motion, stride, and burn a fastball at Paul. The ball sails. He reaches up and across his body for it, the ball whamming into the pocket of the mitt. He grunts. Even forty feet away, I can see him wince.

"Shit, Theresa," he says. "You would've hit the batter in the head, but *shit*."

He and Bob look at each other.

"Kid's got a rifle," Bob says.

I'm thirteen.

I've found my sport.

>>>

Dad wants me to stick with basketball.

"Your problem's not physical, it's mental," he says in the kitchen, leaning against the sink, tapping his forehead with his finger. "It's up here. It could be your ticket to college—"

"I don't really love basketball," I say, sitting glumly at the kitchen table.

"What?"

"I don't like *basketball*," I say louder, raising my eyes to meet his.

My father looks stung, not that I'm insisting I don't like the family game, but that I've openly disagreed with him for the first time ever.

"I have no confidence out there," I say. My legs suddenly shake so violently I fear my knees will thump against the underside of the table. I hadn't meant to confront my dad, hadn't meant to have this conversation at all, but somehow my feelings have rushed out, uncapped and urgent. I swallow, and when I speak again, my voice gets small. "I don't have any fun playing basketball, Dad."

"But you could be so good—"

"You're not hearing me." I practically whisper. My voice feels as if it's trickling away. "It's not my sport. I feel like I let you down when I don't play well because you get mad at me. And when you get mad at me—"

I start to cry. I jerk my hands off my legs and cover my face. "I can't take it when you get mad at me. Because . . ."

I gasp. I can't get the rest out.

I wipe my eyes and nose with the sleeve of Paul's old flannel shirt and breathe so deeply I begin to pant.

"You," I say, then stop, catch my breath, inhale, and my voice becomes stronger and more insistent. "You're *here* with me."

"I try to be," my dad says, his forehead contorted, his look confused. "I try to be here as much as I—"

Frustrated, I lose it and I scream, "You're the only *parent* here with me."

I fall back, breathless, as if the wind had been kicked out of me. "You're all I have."

The tears come again, splashing my face. "I don't have anyone else. I don't have a lot of friends. I need you to . . . be with me . . . to *support* me . . . no matter what."

I can't look at him. I want to flee. I want to disappear. I want to take back what I said. And then I hear a low moan, almost a whimper, and I look up and see that my dad has bent over slightly and he's crying, shielding his face with his hands. I kick the chair back, and I go over to him and bury my head in his chest.

"It's okay, Theresa," he says. "It's okay."

"I'm sorry," I say.

"No, you're right."

I rock slowly in my dad's arms, sniffling, feeling lost and small, as if I'm five years old. Finally he sighs, and I feel him nod as his chin dips. I pull away and breathe, slowly.

"So." He sniffs. "Softball, huh?"

"Yeah." I actually laugh. "I want to pitch."

"You would," he says.

❯❯❯

In the backyard, Dad straps an old mattress to a tree with a couple of Bob's belts and builds a scarecrow next to it. He hires a pitching coach, a sullen geezer with a constant chaw stuffed in one cheek who spits tobacco juice into the paper cup he carries more often than he dispenses pitching advice. Dad fires him and hires Jimmy Moore, a softball legend, allegedly the fastest pitcher in the history of the sport. Jimmy, a quirky surfer type, sees something in me. He introduces an array of pitches into my arsenal— drop balls, curves, risers, changeups, and screwballs. I learn to relax and adjust my grip, and I begin to get the hang of each one. Jimmy shows me how to rock into a methodical rhythm with every pitch, delivering each one with the identical motion, never telegraphing what I'm about to throw. I learn to put on a game face, a stoic mask of nonemotion. I create a pitcher's persona, a different Theresa, steely-eyed and ruthlessly serious, my face shaded beneath my cap, my eyes unblinking in complete concentration.

Over the summer, I join the local park team, then Dad signs me up for a travel team. The girls are older, tougher, and my game improves playing with them and against more experienced competition. The days I'm not playing I practice, either early mornings or evenings until it's too dark to make out the lines of the scarecrow in the backyard. When Dad's not on the road for his work supplying vending machines, he serves as my catcher. Bob, preparing to go off to college at Villanova in Philadelphia, Dad's alma mater, occasionally catches me too. Having learned his lesson by now, he protects his hand by placing a sponge inside the pocket of his catcher's mitt. Paul seems determined to walk his own path, although what that is and where he's going escape me. He becomes a kind of ghost in our lives, a figure in flight, always on the move, spending more time with friends or just *out*. I don't mind. We don't really get along, and he and Dad can't seem to spend two minutes in the same room before one of them loses his temper and Paul, inevitably, storms out.

Freshman year at Seattle Prep, I make the varsity softball team. It doesn't bother me that I will be the only freshman on a team of tight-knit juniors and seniors. I have never really found a niche among girls anywhere, and it looks like I won't be welcomed into this group either. I notice a repeating pattern. Girls gravitate toward those who share their interests, consisting of, in most cases, feeling superior to everyone else (I don't feel that way and never have); clothes (I don't go the mall, and I still shop at Goodwill); or boys (according to Dad and Jimmy, boyfriends steal your focus and make you weak). So once again I'm thrown into the middle of a group of girls to whom I do not relate. It's different now, though. Since my mom died, I have felt lost, everything spinning away, my self-esteem obliterated. I have retreated, mostly by choice, I guess, living my life in the shadows. But with softball, I feel as if I have moved out of the shadows and into the light for the first time. I live a life that's separate, alone, and in softball, by design, on the mound. I am the pitcher. I live on my own island. The team looks to me, relies on me. I have attained what I crave most: control.

I paste a couple of quotes from Michael Jordan above my desk. One says, "I like control." The other says, "Society only acknowledges winners." My dad offers a third maxim: "You've got talent, Theresa. But a lot of people have talent. What will set you apart—what will make you a winner and take you far in life—is your work ethic."

I take all three to heart.

I work harder than anyone. I pitch for hours every day . . . to the scarecrow, to my dad, to the mattress. I run, I stretch, I work out with my brothers' weights. I carpool with one of the catchers on the team, a girl new to the school and a neighbor, and sometimes after school she catches me in the backyard. We become sort of . . . buddies . . . I guess . . . and while I don't become close friends with the girls on the team, we become friend*ly*. It's the first time I ever feel accepted by a group of girls.

It helps that when I pitch I dominate. I've grown to just under six feet tall by the start of the season, and I'm throwing my fastball with increased velocity and my breaking stuff with knee-buckling accuracy. Once we start playing games for real, we pretty much blow away every team in our league on our way to an undefeated season. We draw large crowds to our games, and the local papers take notice of this tall, blond freshman pitching phenom. More than once reporters call me the "new Randy Johnson," comparing me to Seattle's future Hall of Fame pitcher, six-feet-nine-inch Randy Johnson, strikeout master, the Big Unit, the most feared pitcher in the Major Leagues. Flattering, but I can't quite get my head around the hype.

At times, when I lie in bed at night and begin to drift off, thinking about my future and life in general, Mom appears in my dreams, her sweetness and gentleness as real and palpable as a soft breeze on my face. I tell her about softball and my goals, my drive, my need to compete. I tell Mom that I miss her—I miss her like crazy—but I assure her that Dad and I are doing all right. I whisper, "He's doing the best he can," and I tell her that I appreciate him. I tell her not to worry. And then my body shivers, and her face blurs and fades away.

5

CONTROL

GRADES 11–12 / SEATTLE PREP

I MAKE THE NUMBER-ONE TRAVEL SOFTBALL TEAM IN the state of Washington, the gold-level team. I pitch against the best of the best—All-Stars, older girls, tougher girls, girls who've played softball since they were seven years old, girls whose moms and siblings played pro, girls who are training for the Olympics.

I get shelled. The batters I face seem to see the ball coming out of my hand as if it's the size of a beach ball.

I try to adjust. I work slower, I work faster, I practice more. These girls are simply too big, too strong, too experienced, too *good*. One game I get yanked in the third inning. Another time I don't make it out of the first.

I sit dejected on the bench, my head in my hands, my heart thumping in my chest, my breath coming fast as a train. I joined this elite travel team as this hotshot high school pitcher from Se-attle, the new Randy Johnson. Now, a few months later, I just . . . *suck*. I'm so anxious, I can't find the plate. After one ugly outing—hitting a batter, uncorking a wild pitch, allowing two walks and a home run—the coach pulls me. My insides storming, but doing everything I can to appear calm, I place the ball into the coach's hand, sprint into the dugout, and tuck against the wall at the far end of the bench, literally trying to keep my chin up, hoping no one will notice how violently my hands are shaking.

Driving back from this game with my dad, I sink into the passenger seat and moan, "How can I be so good on my school team and suck so bad on the travel team?"

"The girls are better."

"Like *way* better. Like a whole different planet better." I press my face against the window and study the farmland rolling by. "Maybe I'm not cut out for this."

"You know you are," Dad says. He sounds unbelievably calm and not at all concerned. Over these weeks, our car rides to and from games have become my safe place to complain and vent, and Dad has become my therapist, adviser, cheerleader, toughest critic, and, I realize, by default my best friend. Maybe my only friend. "You have to figure it out," he says.

"*How?*" I sigh theatrically. "I can't."

"*Can't,*" Dad says, "is a four-letter word."

I begin to attack the problem from a different angle. I decide that to improve my pitching, I need to give it up. At least temporarily. I stuff my glove in the closet and spend two weeks just working out, getting stronger, running harder, becoming more flexible. Instead of pitching, I *think* about pitching. After two weeks, I dig out my glove, grab my softball, and go to work. I set up Mr. Scarecrow and pitch against the mattress an extra hour a day.

I picture Michael Jordan, whose quotes about control and winning I live by, and I imagine him on the basketball court, his physical superiority and competitive drive matched by his mental toughness. I decide that is what's missing from my game: I need to pitch smart. When I return to pitching in games, I decide not to try to overpower every batter. Instead I try to outthink them. Against a lanky future Olympian, I paint the outside corner with a curveball, waste another curve even farther outside, then come *inside* with a heater, straightening her up, and then I go outside again, causing her to swing clumsily and clunk a weak dribbler to second. I don't succeed this easily all the time, but I make every hitter work. No more vacations in the batter's box when you step in against me. You may hit me, but you will earn it. You may beat me, but I won't beat myself.

》》》

Walking the halls of my high school, I decide, randomly, that I want to go to the junior prom.

I'm not sure why. I don't really have any close friends who are talking about the prom. Well, other than the girls on the softball team, I don't really have any friends, period, and the girls on the team don't appear to be the prom-going type. In the dugout after a game, when I casually float the idea of going to the junior prom as a group, the girls snicker, and when my back is turned, I hear a slew of snide comments. I drop the subject. But I can't stop thinking about the dance.

Two reasons. One, I'd like to participate in some activity at school besides going to class and playing softball. I'd like not to be known as just that "tall jock girl." Two, I'm starting to notice . . . boys. Specifically, I'm starting to notice that boys seem to be noticing me.

I can't put my finger on when I first become aware of this, but I sense eyes on me at various times—entering homeroom before the start of school, in the hallway between classes, in the cafeteria at lunch, and heading across campus after school to softball practice. Guys look at me. You'd have to be blind not to see it. For one thing, I've grown to six feet tall and I've filled out, the way you're supposed to. After a run or a shower I find myself looking in the mirror and liking what I see—tall, trim, lithe, a volleyball player staring back at me. Kind of what I've been going for, the exact body I want. And if I'm honest with myself, I know I work out so that boys *will* notice me.

So I'm not completely shocked when Timothy Fahey, a skinny, pasty-skinned cross-country runner with fire-engine-red hair, a million freckles, and a buzz cut the tip of which doesn't quite reach my chin, asks me to the junior prom. He pops the question one night on the phone after we've gone over some tricky algebra equations. He blurts out his ask, and I respond in a muffled "yeah, sure" and hang up, stunned.

My initial interest in the prom fades, replaced by extreme awkwardness and confusion. For starters, I don't know the first thing about applying makeup, and I have no one to ask for guidance. I flip through magazines looking for advice and tips. I start feeling frustrated, then I feel at a loss. I miss my mom so much. I remember her telling me that even though she wouldn't be here for my prom, her spirit would always be with me. I try to summon her spirit, but all I feel is a deep, crippling loneliness.

I go all DIY for the prom. I choose a pattern for a dress, then, as a trial run, I apply makeup for the first time. I look at myself in the mirror and see a freak staring back at me. I remove the makeup, try again, and gradually get the hang of it.

I make my dress out of a pretty yellow fabric, stopping and starting a dozen times, sometimes wishing I could burn the thing and buy a dress, knowing that Dad would have a hard time justifying buying something I would wear once. I cut it close, but I finish making the dress in time for the dance.

The night of the prom, dress and shoes on, makeup in place, I consider myself in the mirror. Stunned, I blink at my own reflection. My arms are too pale and too muscular, but I have to admit, I don't hate what I see.

You clean up nice, Theresa, I think.

Mom would be proud.

Dad drives me to Timothy's house, where we meet his parents and pose for the obligatory junior prom photo shoot, then Dad drives us to school, Timothy and me sitting on opposite ends of the backseat, our faces pressed against our respective windows. When Dad learned that Timothy had asked me to the prom—my first-ever "date"—Dad not only insisted on being our chauffeur, he also signed up to chaperone the dance. Once there, Timothy and I circulate and hang with kids I know casually from class, then drift over and stand with a group of gangly runners from the cross-country team. The whole time, whether we're dancing or talking, I feel Dad's eyes on me. I don't look in his direction to confirm this; I just sense his presence. What's strange is that I don't feel Dad disapproves or that he's tracking my movements or that he's judging me. I feel that he's protecting me. And I don't mind.

> ❱❱❱

I visit colleges on the east coast. I fall in love with Notre Dame, but the softball coach makes it clear that they will only be able to offer me a partial scholarship. They've been recruiting another pitcher more actively and have made me their second choice. They see me as a work in progress, someone with potential, as opposed to this pitcher who already seems primed to dominate the Big East conference. I smile as the coach relays this information, but my thoughts go dark, and I think, *I really hope I get to pitch against her.* I leave that campus with a sour taste in my mouth, which I later identify as the taste for revenge.

I continue to West Point, where I've been heavily recruited. As I walk through the leafy campus bordered by the Hudson River, I find myself completely taken in by the military environment and the sense of history. I can picture myself here, in uniform, a student preparing to become a soldier.

The problem is the softball team. I don't see myself fitting in with these girls. They seem unwelcoming and cold, colder even than this freezing October night. Not my kind of girls, not my kind of weather. I leave West Point feeling disheartened, wondering if I'll ever find the right fit.

I do. Just outside of Philadelphia.

As soon as I step onto the Villanova campus, I know I've found my home. It helps that my brother Bob, a senior here, is my tour guide and seems to know every student we pass, but I'm completely taken in by the *feel* of the place, dominated by the looming twin spires of Saint Thomas Chapel, with the spirit of Saint Augustine, the founding order, permeating the campus. It helps even more that the coach of the softball team has been following my high school career and has watched my steady progress on the travel team. She sees me as the anchor of a team she's gearing up to make a statement in the Big East conference.

"So, we play Notre Dame?"

"They're our rivals," the coach says.

Oh, I want in.

Villanova offers me a scholarship for softball, and I eagerly sign the forms.

And yet . . . I can't shake the powerful feeling that overcame me when I toured West Point.

"Go ROTC," my brother Bob says. "Do the Marine Corps option like I did. Go for a scholarship too. It's cake. Basically a fitness test. You'll rock it."

"But wait, ROTC and softball? Can I do both?"

"I have a friend who was a triathlete and tried out for the Olympics while she was in the Marine Corps. You can definitely do both. And if you score both scholarships? It's a full ride plus pay. It's like you go to college and make money on the deal."

I apply for the ROTC scholarship. I have to run three miles in twenty-one minutes, do one hundred sit-ups in two minutes, and hold a flexed-arm hang on a pull-up bar for seventy seconds.

Bob's right. Cake.

I commit to Villanova, receiving a full ride with two scholarships. But I still have to finish high school.

>>>

A second-semester senior now, I'm basically running out the clock. School has become a time suck, each day a replica of the day before. I drift from class to class, take my seat in what feels like slow motion, spending half of every period battling to stay awake. In precalculus, a course that interests me not at all, the teacher, Mr. Clark, relies on an overhead projector to put up problems in front of the class. Except that once he hits the lights, between the hum of the projector and Mr. Clark's reedy voice, I'm asleep in seconds. Recently Mr. Clark moved me to the front row, his futile attempt to keep me awake.

One day, as the calming slosh from a wave of sleep carts me away, I hear the distant sound of laughing. I nod off again, then I feel one of Mr. Clark's scuffed brown Weejuns nudging my boot. I jerk awake.

"Theresa?"

"Yes?"

"Can you solve the problem on the overhead?"

I sit up, peer at the screen, and read, "Theresa, will you go to prom with me?"

"Oh my God," I say, to an explosion of laughter.

"That's from me," a voice says. Guy in the last row, waving his hand. Donald Bailey. Slicked-back hair. Glasses. Cross-country team. I wave back. What is it with me and skinny long-distance runners?

"Well?" Mr. Clark says. "The suspense is killing us."

I really have no choice. "Sure," I say, reddening, as the class applauds.

For some bizarre reason, the two last weeks of senior year improve socially. Donald's group of friends welcomes me, and we all pitch in and rent a limo for the prom. My dad again chaperones, but this time he doesn't seem quite so intrusive. Or maybe since I've been invited suddenly into a social circle, I don't notice him as much. The prom turns out to be your typical overheated, alcohol-infused evening in three acts—the before party, the prom itself, and the after party held at a top-secret location that everybody knows. I watch the comings and goings from a slightly detached perspective, an uninvolved bystander with Donald, my skinny runner date, by my side.

We hold graduation at the Seattle Opera House downtown, and to my surprise, I'm called to the stage three times—to receive my ROTC scholarship, a Jesuit secondary education award, and a plaque for Athlete of the Year. By the third presentation, I feel slightly embarrassed and a little giddy. The class then settles in for the valedictorian's speech by Becky Clinton, a girl I call a friend even though we don't hang out that much because I'm always playing softball and Becky's always studying or playing soccer. Her speech, which is brilliant (Becky goes on to MIT and eventually becomes a pediatric orthopedic surgeon), includes a reference to *me*. She talks about my work ethic, my passion and dedication to my sport, and my genuine concern for those who have experienced hardship or loss. I'm shocked and very touched. Now, even more than feeling included, I feel as if I have been *seen*, and that I have been all along.

After graduation, the senior class pulls an all-nighter, starting at the Space Needle and ending on a boat that lazily sails the harbor until dawn. We embrace our class theme, "Let's Party Like It's 1999," because, well, it *is* 1999, and we are partying hard. But the quote that sticks in my head is one my Dad taught me years ago: "It's not how you start; it's how you finish."

6

WILDCAT

I STUFF EVERYTHING I'M TAKING TO COLLEGE INTO A canvas seabag borrowed from my brother Bob and check it curbside at Seattle International Airport. The next morning, after a day of travel and a nervous night in a hotel, Dad and I head to campus. Outside my dorm, I watch every other incoming freshman arrive in a U-Haul truck, a car hauling a U-Haul trailer, or an SUV stuffed to the gills with suitcases. Kids and parents unload their vehicles and trucks and load up multiple plastic bins with their belongings. I am the only freshman arriving with exactly one bag.

My dad and I locate my room, and I claim one of the beds by tossing my seabag onto it. Moments later, the door swings open, and a short, adorable fireball with jet-black hair charges in. She pauses in the doorway and takes me in. I'm a head taller than she is. Her eyes bulge. "Theresa?"

I nod, frozen.

Kelly throws her arms around me, pulls back, and cranes her head up. "We could be sisters," she says.

As it turns out, we will be.

Moved into my room, I walk Dad to his rental car. For the first time in two days, I feel like I can breathe, and then I'm instantly overcome with homesickness. I don't want to feel this now. I want to bury this feeling and suck it up. Show my dad I'm tough. I can handle this. I'm eighteen and moving on with my life. I want to feel strong and independent, but I can't ward off feeling shell shocked and immensely sad.

I bite my lip and study the pavement of the visitors' parking lot. I can feel that I'm about five seconds from a meltdown.

"Well, okay," my dad says, avoiding my eyes as I avoid his. I know at once that he feels the same loss as I do, or at least the enormity of this impending sea change. His sons both inducted into the Marine Corps, his daughter across the country in college, his beloved wife gone, I picture him solemnly returning to the emptiest of nests.

"It's going to be great," he says.

"I'll call," I say, throwing my arms around him. I pull away, kiss him on the cheek, and head toward the dorm, my new home. I pivot when I'm almost at the front door. He stands next to his rental car, suddenly looking very small. He waves and I wave back. I turn away, power through the doors and into the downstairs lobby, my head down so he won't see me cry.

In my new world—this freshman dorm full of girls from every state and several foreign countries, in addition to my roommate Kelly—I fall in with two more women, who become my close friends.

First Heather, who lives down the hall, a blonde, blue-eyed ROTC sign-up who embodies the term *put together*. She fusses over makeup and hair and chooses her clothes and nail polish with precision and purpose. Although she never announces this officially, Heather makes me her pet project when it comes to all things feminine.

The second, Kriste Romano, I had met over the summer when playing travel ball. She is a short (well, every girl at Villanova is short compared to me), quiet, olive-skinned, dark-haired Italian beauty who lives two floors above me and who has also come to school on a softball scholarship. Kriste has been recruited as a catcher, and we bond immediately. We're so crazy in sync that we bump into each other in the mailroom one morning and discover that our mailboxes are next to each other. I introduce Kriste to Kelly and Heather, and we form a Fearsome Foursome, friends met the first week of freshman year, friends made for life.

>>>

On the first day of school—and for six weeks after—I am in ROTC indoctrination, what we call in-doc, a fancy way of saying boot camp. I wake at five-thirty in the morning, throw on clothes, and meet Heather by the dorm elevators. We jog across campus to the athletic field, just in time for the in-doc that goes from six until seven-thirty. Our instructor kicks our butts, running us hard, and on the first day calls out Heather for showing up with blue nail polish. At seven-thirty, sore, sweaty, our muscles throbbing, we race back to our dorms, shower frantically, and then Kriste and I haul ass to German, our eight-thirty class, held in a classroom on the top floor of the tallest building on campus. At the end of the class day, I rush back to my dorm, change again, and meet

Kriste for softball practice. Another shower, a fast dinner, then to the library or the dorm lounge to study until I'm so exhausted I practically crawl back to my room and crash, usually before midnight. When the six weeks of in-doc ends, Kriste agrees to work out with me every morning to keep in shape for softball. We give ourselves an extra hour of sleep and meet at six-thirty. I'm determined to maintain the discipline I gained from in-doc. Kriste's all in too, although more than once she shows up for our workout still wearing her Flintstone pajamas.

On the softball team, two lowly freshman grunts relegated to the bench and regularly hazed, Kriste and I cling to each other, our relationship cementing even more. We're outliers who just don't fit in with the other girls on the team, most of whom drink and party hard and often. Kriste and I explain, sheepishly, that we don't drink and that we take school kind of seriously. The juniors and seniors on the team eye us suspiciously and with distaste, as if we consider ourselves superior to them because we actually *study*. Then, at one of the first team meetings, someone on the team announces that we're required to watch an important training video. She hits the lights, and instead of girls playing softball, up comes midget porn. The other girls holler and cheer, including the other freshmen, but Kriste and I, grossed out and uncomfortable, walk out of the room. After that, the older girls on the team see us as boring and beneath them, ordering us to carry the team's bulging canvas bags of bats and balls to and from the practice field, and to clean up the field after practice.

Coach Q—tall, pale, red-headed and serious—doesn't seem to notice any of this. Despite being recruited as the anchor of the pitching staff, I'm hardly ever called on to pitch, except to mop up for an inning or two after a game has gotten out of reach in either a crushing loss or a lopsided win. Kriste receives the same treatment; we're considered, for better or worse, a unit. One day, sitting by ourselves at the end of the bench in the dugout, I reach into my backpack and pull out a stack of flashcards with our German vocabulary words. We decide if we're not going to play, we might as well study. We test each other with flashcards, grilling each other before weekly current events quizzes, even scribbling first drafts of term papers. Eventually someone on the team busts us, and Coach Q banishes us to the bull pen to practice pitching, which we do, for ten minutes, then we get to work on our homework.

By midsemester, I'm struggling—fighting to find my place on the softball team, wondering if I belong on this team at all, fearing I'll fail out of school, and experiencing constant, crippling stabs of homesickness. I call my Dad almost every day and wail about how unhappy I am. He tells me to hang in, that the transition from high school to college is hard and he promises it will get better. I talk about transferring to a school that will offer me a chance to pitch meaningful innings and not crush me academically. Kriste refuses to entertain even the slightest notion of quitting. She can't give up her scholarship, the only way she can afford to continue at college. I decide I will stick it out for her, if not for myself.

During this time, I develop an annoying habit—a tic, I guess you'd call it—that seems to irritate everyone, my ROTC instructors and Coach Q especially. When Coach Q talks to me, if I'm overtired or don't agree with what she says, I roll my eyes. I'm honestly unaware that I do this, but after the first time I roll my eyes, she says, "Oh, you don't agree?"

"What? I'm sorry, I didn't—"

"You know what? You have an attitude. And I don't appreciate it."

"I didn't say anything—"

"You're on a team, I'm the coach, and you do what I say. I don't care if you don't like it."

She storms off. I look at Kriste.

Eye roll.

><><><

My homesickness has on more than one lonely night driven me to tears in the library or in my room in front of my computer. I know, too, that sometimes I just feel crappy from lack of sleep and eating horribly. Determined to avoid the so-called "freshman fifteen," I commit to eating salads and fruit as much as possible. But after a few days of eating this way, I feel famished and spend the next few days binging on burgers or pizza. This yo-yo eating depresses me. But mostly, I just feel lonely. I tell this to Dad.

"I've been lonely, too," he says. "Plus I miss watching your games. I've decided to rent a place in Philly and check out job opportunities."

I'm so relieved. I need my dad.

Second semester, my dad finds a room in a house near campus. I spend a few nights a week studying at his place, sometimes with Kriste. When I don't feel like dragging myself back to my dorm, I stay over. One night, as I prepare to head back to campus, he says he has some news. He has applied to the seminary. My dad has decided to become a priest.

>>>

I call for a meeting with Coach Q after the season ends. I sit across from her and study my hands, which have been shaking since I walked in the door. "I'm transferring," I say.

Coach Q's mouth tightens into a thin line. "You're leaving Villanova?"

"Yes." I shift in my seat. I feel my throat constrict. I sit on my hands to steady them. "I came here to play softball."

I let that statement hang in the air between us for a long beat mainly because I'm so nervous, then I say, "I'm not playing, so . . ."

"You're only a freshman."

"I don't think that should matter." I soften my voice. "I know what I can do. You recruited me to be a starting pitcher, not to throw meaningless innings when we're way ahead or way behind. I'm better than that." I clear my throat. "I came here full of confidence. I've lost that. I need to be in a situation where I can get it back."

Coach Q makes a teepee with her fingers and considers me. "Not many freshmen—not many students, period—would confront me the way you're doing right now."

"I just want to pitch," I say, my voice squeaking.

"Tell you what." Coach Q leans forward. "You bust your butt this summer, improve your breaking stuff, and I'll strongly consider making you a starter. Deal?"

She offers her hand. I shake it.

"Thank you," I say.

"You may not believe it, but that was my plan all along."

A week later, our team attends the Big East conference annual awards banquet. Over a dinner of rubber chicken and mushy vegetables, we applaud politely as students from other schools collect gleaming glass plaques for winning the Big East Championship—our rival Notre Dame wins this year, we finish second—the Big East's Most Valuable Player, Rookie of the Year, and the award that interests me most, the Big East Pitcher of the Year. The winner, who weaves her way from the seat at her table to the podium on the stage, is the pitcher Notre Dame recruited instead of me. She thanks her teammates and coaches, sniffles through a loving tribute to her family, then holds her plaque triumphantly above her head.

I'm gonna bust my butt and become a starter, I think. *I'm gonna be the one standing up there.*

7

FIT FOREVER

2000–2007

I FEEL UGLY.

With two weeks left to freshman year, as finals loom, I walk through life feeling moody and *gross*. I've fought off the freshman fifteen, but I can't seem to stop yo-yoing between salads, fruits, and healthy snacks and burgers, pizza, and desserts, often late at night. When I do manage to stick to salads, I feel faint within two hours. Sometimes I eat, and sometimes I just starve and then feel so depressed I go to bed ridiculously early, by nine o'clock. I face the wall so Kelly can't see me and softly cry myself to sleep.

For distraction, I lose myself leafing through fitness magazines like *Shape*, *Oxygen*, and *Outside*. I fantasize about looking like the models on the covers and in the photo spreads. I particularly identify with superstar volleyball player and sports fashion model

Gabrielle Reece, who is about my height, six feet one, and totally buff. She clearly works out, but she must also monitor what she eats. I look in the mirror and compare myself to her. I don't see a volleyball player's body staring back at me. I see a young woman with ghostly pale skin, bulging muscles, and hair that I hate. I vow to change my appearance, somehow.

My brother Paul provides the answer.

Back in Seattle over the summer—my dad has kept the family house—I explain that I'm frustrated by the way I've eaten all freshman year. I need to find a way of eating that might actually help me improve my performance as a pitcher.

"I know a way to get really fit and lean," Paul says. "We can all do it."

He shows us the website for the "Fit Forever" program, which specifies exactly what to eat for six straight days followed by a seventh "free day," allowing you to eat anything you want. The website encourages us to enter a twelve-week competition. You simply provide before and after photos, write a short narrative telling your personal story, and keep a weekly weight loss diary. The top prize winners receive $5,000, a cool-looking suede jacket, and most intriguing to me, a photo shoot for a fitness magazine. As we check out the program online, my dad brightens. He's put on a few pounds since moving to Philadelphia and sees our family competition as motivation. I don't want to be left out. The three of us enter the Fit Forever contest.

On our first six controlled-eating days, my brother and I awake early, go for a run, hit the free weights, and follow our Fit Forever meals and supplements to the letter. On our first free day, we go crazy. We drive to the market and load our shopping cart with cookies and ice cream. At dinnertime, we order two large pizzas and gorge ourselves. After devouring nearly a gallon of ice cream between us, we lie inert on the living room floor, moaning like a couple of beached whales. I sleep late the next morning, and when I finally roll out of bed, I feel marginally better, especially when I return to the Fit Forever diet—back to day one of the six-day plan. As the week goes on, I start dreading the upcoming free day. By the time the seventh day arrives, I'm so hungry that I pig out again, even though I know I shouldn't. That night I'm once again sick and listless, this time feeling dizzy and nauseated. I wake up the next morning drained and ruined, as if I had a massive hangover. But I battle through the seventh-day blues. Three weeks into Fit Forever and my daily workouts with Paul, I start to see a difference. My body has become tighter, and I feel hot-wired, bristling with energy.

>>>

I leave Seattle in early July and head to San Diego as part of my ROTC duty, completing four weeks of intense midshipman training. I train in a helicopter, shoot mortars, spend a day on a nuclear submarine, and fly in an F-18. At the same time, I do my best to stick to the Fit Forever meal plan and maintain my workout schedule. Strangely, these four weeks of ROTC training settle me down. I feel at home in this military environment. I also know that eyes are on me. I've dyed my hair blonde, dominate when I work out, and ace the obstacle course. As I stride in my crisp Navy uniform, I experience a kind of rush, a jolt of self-confidence. The women seem intimidated, and with a secret smile, I imagine the men thinking, *I love a woman in uniform.*

In August, I return home to Seattle and spend my days working out and pitching, two, three hours a day, punishing the mattress in the backyard. As summer ends, the family disperses. Paul has returned to duty, Dad moves to the seminary in Boston, and I go back to my dorm in Villanova, now in a single room where I will live alone.

I ratchet up my workouts and devote myself to Fit Forever. I start to notice an even more marked difference in my body. I no longer look like the flabby college freshman who posed for my Fit Forever "before" photo. I've become a nineteen-year-old Marine option, tall, thin, tight, and *ripped*, closer to achieving my ideal, a Gabrielle Reece volleyball body. And I'm not the only one who notices this.

At softball, several of my teammates hover around after practice as I help gather stray equipment. Casually, they comment on how great I look. Did I hire a trainer? Did I go to a special summer fitness camp? One player wonders if I underwent some kind of *procedure* . . . liposuction or something. I tell them about Fit Forever and our family competition. Intrigued, several sign up. Soon we form two teams within the team, those dedicated to softball only and those committed to Fit Forever. Already the strongest member of the team, I now feel like a fitness guru.

Meanwhile, Coach Q keeps her promise. She pencils me into the pitching rotation and, after I dominate our first intersquad scrimmage, names me the team's number-one starter. I feel both pride and pressure, and I seem to get even less sleep than the year before. I had imagined I would cruise as a sophomore. Not even close. My life virtually redlines as I attempt to juggle studying, softball, working out, Fit Forever, and ROTC. Then, with no room in my life at all, I add, ridiculously, one more thing.

My first boyfriend.

I meet "Carl" during a Philadelphia area ROTC paintballing exercise. Carl, also doing the Marine option, goes to Penn and seeks me out after the exercise. Although I'd been hit on during freshman year by several guys, most of them gangly, dopey baseball players deemed unworthy by my protective shield of Kriste, Kelly, and Heather, Carl seems different. For one thing, he's smart. For another, he's a fitness freak and martial arts maniac.

We end up flirting after the paintballing exercise. Well, *he* flirts. I try to flirt, but I'm sure I sound ridiculous. I nod a lot and giggle girlishly. I guess I'm not a total turnoff because he asks me out for Saturday night.

Carl invites me to dinner at his place. He makes tuna fish sandwiches and offers me cookie dough batter for dessert. I eat politely, anxious about ingesting a bunch of garbage for my Fit Forever free day and fearing that I'll feel sick and gross in the morning. After we eat, Carl goes on about his obsession with martial arts and demonstrates a couple of choke holds, an excuse, I realize, to get his hands on me. He reveals that he's really getting to like me, so much so that for us to go out, he has rescheduled the regular weekly meeting of his Dungeons and Dragons club.

Later, back at the dorm, dissecting the date, my posse, as I'd predicted, writes Carl off the moment I tell them about the tuna fish sandwiches and choke holds.

"No way this guy's a keeper," Heather says. We all agree.

Which is why I only stay with Carl for three months.

I call Carl a decent starter boyfriend, no more. By Thanksgiving, we're pretty much done, but it takes another month of his canceling a bunch of dates and radio silence before I officially call it quits over Christmas break. After not hearing from him for a couple of weeks, I go to Penn, knock on his door, and confront him. He's so stunned to see me, he turns white. He stammers and invites me in, but I explain I've only come by to tell him to his face that he was beyond rude to end all communication with me as if I didn't exist. He mumbles a lame apology, then I level him. "The truth is, Carl, you just weren't cutting it."

>>>

Over Christmas break, the whole family gathers in Seattle. We follow our strict Fit Forever guidelines, then on the first free day I bake a batch of cookies. As I slide the tray out of the oven, the phone rings. Of course, none of the guys in this house bothers answering it, so, annoyed and moody, I whip off my oven mitt and grunt a pissed-off "hello" into the phone.

A guy's voice on the line hesitates. "Theresa Hornick?"

"Yes?"

"I'm calling from Fit Forever," the guy says and gives his name. "I just wanted to tell you, Theresa, that your before and after photos show a dramatic contrast. You look absolutely amazing. You're one of our top finishers. You came in second out of fifteen thousand entries in your category."

"What?"

"Who is that?" Paul asks, snatching a warm cookie, my dad and Bob clomping right behind him.

I cup my hand over the phone and mouth, "Fit Forever. I won second place in my category."

"Ooh-rah!" Paul shouts.

"Wow," I say back into the phone. "That's awesome. I'm . . . shocked."

The guy starts rattling off my prizes—the check for five thousand dollars, the leather jacket, and the professional photo shoot. As he explains how to claim my prizes, I nod dumbly and look over at my family. They seem frozen in a tableau in our kitchen. I suddenly feel happy and validated for *them*. We began Fit Forever as a family competition. I consider this a family victory.

"I'm very happy about this," I hear myself say. "But my dad deserves it more than I do. After my mom died, he took care of everyone but himself. He got heavy, let himself go. Since we all started Fit Forever, he's lost forty pounds, but what's more is he got his life back. He's the real winner."

Silence on the other end of the phone.

Finally, the guy says, "That's wonderful. Unfortunately, he didn't finish in the top three in his category—"

I don't really concentrate on what he says next. I do hear a few details about the photo shoot, the time and place, and something about wetsuits and a bikini on a beach. When we hang up, Dad throws his arms around me and tells me how proud he is, and Bob and Paul punch me repeatedly on my arms, a touching show of affection, then we celebrate, all of us gorging ourselves on the spoils of victory—the tray of warm, moist chocolate chip cookies that will make me feel sick later.

❯❯❯

Second semester of sophomore year, I move out of my single room and back in with Kelly. At the same time, my posse spreads the news: I have become a fitness model, soon to appear in a national magazine. Heather, serving as both fashion consultant and chaperone, arranges to attend the photo shoot with me at Virginia Beach during a long weekend. Meanwhile, wowed by how I look—lean, buff, and seriously in shape—almost every remaining member of the softball team signs up for Fit Forever. Prior to opening day, Coach Q officially names me our number one starter, and for most of the season, I pitch lights out. I earn Academic All-America and Second Team All Big East honors, a huge step up from spending freshman year wallowing in the bull pen going over German vocabulary words with Kriste.

Sophomore year ends, and I head to California for an ROTC commitment: Marine Air Ground Training Command, two weeks of hell baking in the Mojave Desert, where the temperature reaches 120 degrees by noon every day. I come back exhausted and injured. My right eye has swollen shut, the result of an infection I've contracted from funnels of hot sand blowing into my face. Undaunted, I go back across the country to Stratford, Connecticut, where I'll be playing summer ball for softball legend John Stratton and his renowned Raybestos Brakettes. John takes one look at me and sends me to the team doctor, who prescribes antibiotic eye drops and fits me with an eye patch.

I try to pitch with the patch. If possible, I've gotten even stronger this summer, and I've discovered extra velocity on my fastball. Unfortunately, I can't see a thing and John relegates me to pitching batting practice. My pitches sail over batters' heads, soar behind them, or land two feet in front of them. The hitters routinely cover their heads or dance as if they're being shot at.

One day, during a workout in the gym, I notice that blood is leaking through the back of my workout pants. I head to the locker room, slide my pants down, twist to look at myself in the mirror, and see an oozing, bloody cyst on my butt. I return to the doctor, who prescribes medicated baths and a patch for my butt cyst. I limp back to the baseball diamond, half-blind, my butt patched and throbbing in pain. That night, soaking in the tub to soothe my sorrowful ass, I decide to shave my legs. The razor slips and I slice my leg practically down to the shin bone.

"What the hell happened to you?" John says the next day as I show up to practice wearing an eye patch, a bulging bandage on my butt, and another bandage practically swathing my leg. "Did you get into a knife fight?"

"I'm having a bad week," I say.

"I can see that. Listen, starting Saturday we hit the heart of our schedule—six games a week and a bunch of Sunday doubleheaders. You're pitching. So do me a favor and get better. Today you can coach first base."

Great.

I get to stand on my one good leg in the sticky Connecticut humidity, flicking away ravenous mosquitoes while instructing base runners when to take off for second and when to stop halfway and hustle back to the bag. I kick the dirt and squint at the few spectators who've come to watch the game. We've drawn a sparse crowd, mostly single women with short haircuts wearing jeans and work shirts. And one guy my age. Why is he here? Is he related to somebody on the team? He can't be checking us out. No way he's checking *me* out. I'm like the only straight woman on the team, and I'm blind and bleeding.

Shit. He *is* checking me out.

The Brakettes take the field, and the few dozen people in the bleachers stand and cheer, and this guy, camped behind first base, whistles with two fingers and shouts, "Go, Theresa!"

I kick the dirt again. I prowl the length of the first-base coach's box, clap my hands, shout encouragement to our leadoff hitter, and turn slightly to get another look at the guy who whistled at me and called my name.

He's kind of cute, actually.

And now he smiles.

And I—shyly—smile back.

Over the weekend, the team doctor removes my eye patch, pronounces my cyst practically cleared up, and announces that the gash on my leg is healing nicely and probably won't leave a scar. He clears me to pitch.

I take the mound on Sunday, complete my warm-up tosses, consult with my catcher, and toe the rubber. As I do, I nonchalantly glance toward the first-base side of the bleachers. He's there. My biggest fan. Standing, whistling, waving.

I go into my windup and burn a fastball over the outside corner, freezing the batter. Strike one. I peek toward the stands. My fan's smiling, giving me two thumbs up. I tip my cap.

We win in extra innings. As I gather my stuff and start to exit the field, my fan waits for me by the far end of the dugout. I fight off an attack of shyness and walk over to him.

"Good game," he says. He's taller than I thought, almost exactly my height, and even cuter closer up.

"Thanks," I say, extending my hand. "I'm Theresa."

"I know," he says. "I've watched you play a few times."

"I know," I say.

Now he grins shyly. "I'm Ivan," he says.

"Ivan," I say, trying it on.

"It's Russian."

"Wow. Russian. What are you doing in Connecticut?"

"I'm in med school."

You know, I kinda like this guy.

Off the field, I maintain my rigid workout regimen while Ivan and I become an item. One Saturday night, he takes me to meet his parents, old-country Russians who barely speak English.

"*Your girlfriend is so strong,*" his mom says to him in Russian.

"*Very big muscles,*" his dad says in Russian.

"*Hopefully she will not become stronger than you,*" his mother says in Russian.

"What was that about?" I ask Ivan later.

"My parents are concerned that you're stronger than me," he says.

"I've never heard that one before." I laugh, assuming he'll laugh with me. He doesn't. He looks genuinely concerned.

"Maybe you should lighten up a bit with the weights," he says.

"Are you kidding me?"

"Well, you are pretty . . . muscular. I'm not saying I don't like it. I'm just saying, maybe, for my parents' sake—"

I shut him down for the rest of that night. He calls me the next day and apologizes. But I notice that after that Saturday night with his parents, we reduce the number of dates that involve weight training.

I like Ivan, but his parents make me extremely self-conscious. I've already started to question the way I look, and now thanks to them I feel like the largest woman alive.

Which is why I stay with him for only five months.

8

MY FIRST TIME

IT HAPPENS THE FIRST TIME DURING CHRISTMAS break, when I'm at home with the family in Seattle.

Still following Fit Forever, we all go off the plan for our free day, eating anything we want for Christmas dinner. Bob and Paul, notoriously huge eaters, devour everything that lands on their plates within seconds. It's almost as if they're having an eating contest. I don't want to be left out of that. I'm all about competition. I can eat as much as they can. I go for it.

I'm not sure exactly when I lose control. It may be after my third helping of turkey, mashed potatoes, and gravy. Or maybe it comes after my second wedge of pecan pie topped with a snowdrift of whipped cream. I know that at some point I start to lose myself . . . literally lose *myself*. This Theresa, the one so conscious of what and how much I eat, the Fit Forever Theresa, evaporates.

I'm only vaguely aware of eating yet another slice of pie, and then I feel . . . sick. Beyond sick. I feel overcome. And then I feel stabbing pain.

I push away from the table, walk out of the room, and go into the bathroom. I lock the door, lift the toilet seat, and then the sickness overtakes me, capsizes me, and I . . . throw up.

I don't plan it. I don't do anything to make myself vomit. It just happens. It seems strangely natural. And I feel instantly better. I feel relieved. The pain ebbs and dissolves. I return to the table and look at the food piled up on plates and platters and hear my brothers laughing, their voices roaring, deafening, so loud and violent I want to slam my hands over my ears. I stare at all the food in front of me, and I feel disgusted, nauseated, and distant. I try to snap out of this daze, this near trance. Finally I come back to earth and force myself to glance at my dad. He's looking directly at me, his eyes doused with worry.

>>>

When I return to school, I make an appointment with a counselor at the health center. I want to talk to someone because I feel so confused. The girls on the softball team, friends, even people I barely know consider me the campus fitness queen, the girl so fit she's appeared in magazines, the person you turn to for workout advice and, ironically, how to eat. That's how they see me. But I don't feel that way at all. Instead I feel fierce pressure that I put on myself, followed by lacerating anxiety. I critique my body viciously, unsparingly, an inner voice dripping with sarcasm hounding me: *Look at you, Theresa. You're fat. Disgusting. The way you eat? You've blown it. You're back to square one. All your hard work? Down the toilet. You're no fitness guru. You're a fraud.*

The counselor I meet, sweet, eager, well-intentioned but spectacularly out of her league, suggests that I may be struggling with a condition she calls *disordered eating*. That's about as far as she can go. Dr. Young doesn't offer much in the way of helpful advice—she doesn't really seem to know what to do—but for the rest of junior year she at least provides me with a kind, sympathetic ear, and she does offer one helpful tip.

In general, we talk about control issues, eating issues, and the sometimes troubling rigidity of Fit Forever. After a particularly stressful week, when my eating seems to be both spinning out of control and controlling me, I ask Dr. Young, "How can I de-stress? How can I lighten up?"

"You have to go easier on yourself," she says, then suggests I keep a journal. She tells me to write down my thoughts and feelings without censoring myself, every day if I can, and so I do. I write about Coach Q's mood swings and why the boyfriends I choose don't seem to cut it. I also write about my increasingly complicated relationship with food and particularly what I fear may be turning into an addiction: my relationship with Fit Forever.

As usual, the softball team heads to Florida for spring break. We stay at a hotel that serves freshly baked cookies in the lobby every night. I can't eat enough of these cookies—chocolate chip and oatmeal—and I gorge myself. I go out of control, becoming a tall, blond Cookie Monster, shoving cookie after cookie into my mouth, devouring them almost whole.

The next morning, I feel sick and hung over and overdosed on sugar, and I can't pitch. Coach Q pulls me after two innings. Disgusted with myself, I rush off the field, duck into the dugout, and curl up in the corner on the bench. My chest heaving, I fight to keep from screaming. I'm a junior, our number one starting pitcher, on the brink of having a spectacular season, minus today, and I need to be able to harness my emotions, at least outwardly. I need to be more . . . *in control.* I tell myself, *Theresa, you can't show this shit to the team.*

From that moment on, I bottle up my emotions. I keep my spirits high, even when I'm feeling down or disgusted. In other words, I fake it.

>>>

My birthday approaches—April 28, a landmark birthday, my twenty-first. I have become legal. All my friends agree: I should have a party, and I should *drink*. At first I shoot down the idea. I'm more than a little concerned about hosting an on-campus party with alcohol, but everyone assures me that we'll have a very small gathering at our apartment and limit the invitations to the inner circle and my brother Paul, who's back stateside.

My brother flies in from Sacramento, arrives at my apartment, throws himself and his gear on the couch, and takes up residence in the living room the way a redwood might fit into a flower pot. Paul, six feet seven and massive, intimidates, well, *everyone.* As promised, a small group gathers at our apartment, and then we travel as a pack to the Cheesecake Factory for my birthday dinner. On the way I tell Paul I will have exactly one drink.

"I'm pitching tomorrow against UConn," I say. "It's an important league game. We can't afford to lose."

"Fine, one drink, Little Sis," he says. "A couple at most."

I do have one drink, but I eat too much and go to bed feeling like shit. Paul, the pied piper, leads a troop of people back to the apartment and stays up until I have no idea when, drinking with I have no idea who. I wake up groggy and nervous. I'm always nervous before I pitch, but today I feel shaky. I get dressed and find Paul passed out on the couch. Going on nervous energy overload, I recycle the empties scattered all over the apartment, wash the dishes left in the sink, bundle up and dump the trash, and head out for the game.

The game starts, and I just cannot find a rhythm. Suddenly all my nervous energy dissolves and I feel slow, listless. My legs feel thick and heavy, as if they're stuck in quicksand. Kriste tries everything she can think of to snap me out of my lethargy—speeding me up, slowing me down, telling me a joke, dishing about girls we know, even shouting at me. Nothing helps. I allow a run in the first, two in the second, another in the third. After I walk the first two batters in the fourth, Coach Q hoists herself out of the dugout and jogs to the mound, joining Kriste and me for what I dread most, a conversation.

I keep my eyes pinned on the ground as Coach Q says, "What's going on with you today?"

I shrug.

"It was her twenty-first birthday yesterday," Kriste says. "That can throw you off."

"Wow, great, happy birthday," Coach Q says. "Now listen, we're only one run down, so snap out of this. I want you to concentrate on—"

I see her lips moving but I cannot make out one word she's saying. I can only hear her voice, flat and hollow, as if trapped inside a tin drum. I strain to listen, but all I can think is *When will she leave me alone?*

"You got that?" Coach Q asks.

I nod.

She pats me on the butt and sprints back toward the dugout.

"That was inspiring," Kriste says.

My eyes drift to a commotion in the stands behind home plate. Paul, wearing wraparound shades, clambers down the steps and plants himself onto an aisle seat. He points a finger at me. I point back.

"The Marines have landed," I say, shooting him a proud smile.

I pitch well the rest of the game, but even though we're only down one run, we can't get to their pitcher, and we drop the game to UConn, my first loss of the season.

"Well, that sucked," I say to Kriste as we leave the field.

"Yeah, but you know what didn't suck? You pulled yourself together, and you pitched really well even though you didn't have your best stuff. You gutted it out."

"Thanks, but we didn't win."

"We should have. Wasn't your fault. None of us could hit." Kriste eyes me, hesitates, and then says, "You're unbelievably tough, Theresa. Never forget that."

Despite the blip that is the UConn game, I continue to dominate. Even so, we finish second in the Big East, once again coming in behind Notre Dame. Our team again attends the league banquet. I stick to the Fit Forever meal plan, barely touching anything on my plate, feeling fidgety and strangely feverish, so much so that it almost doesn't register when the speaker at the podium announces the 2002 "Big East Pitcher of the Year" and says my name, and applause rolls through the banquet hall. *Wait, what?* I'd assumed that the pitcher from the Big East champion, Notre Dame, would win again, but now I recover from my strange fever state, and just in case my name has escaped from the person's mouth at the podium by mistake, I run to the stage to accept my gleaming glass plaque. I start speaking spontaneously—I haven't prepared any kind of speech—thanking my teammates, my dad, my brothers, John Stratton, Coach Q, the assistant coaches, my teammates. Then I look at Kriste, and I say, "I would never have won this award without my catcher, Kriste Romano, who makes me look good every game. Thank you." Clutching my award, I jog off the stage. I hold the plaque high and allow my teammates to swallow me up at my seat. And for one tiny instant, I see my mom's face, and she's smiling.

>>>

As part of my ROTC commitment, I spend six weeks in Quantico, Virginia, in the swampy humidity of summer, attending Marine Corps Officer Candidates School (OCS). I bunk in a barracks with an all-female platoon—forty-five women, all of us shoehorned into one hot, smelly room.

The day begins at dawn as we dress, line up, disperse, and go through daily physical fitness training—exercises, an obstacle course, a run or hike in full uniform and pack. Sergeant instructors drill us, abuse us, train us. In the afternoons, clumped together in musty, cramped classrooms without air conditioning, we work on projects or listen to lectures on strategies and tactics. As our instructors drone on in front of the class, I invariably fall asleep in the back row. By the end of the six weeks, my sides and legs are bruised purple from officer candidates elbowing me and kicking me to keep me awake.

At one point, I'm assigned the role of platoon commander for the day. I rock the early morning physical fitness regimen, but I struggle getting my platoon to listen to me. One sergeant instructor, Sergeant Spikes, whose name I've misheard and whom I mistakenly call Sergeant Pyle, takes me aside.

"You aced the obstacle course, Hornick," Sergeant Spikes says. "But you have to speak louder."

"Yes, Sergeant Instructor."

"Did you hear me?"

"Yes, Sergeant Instructor."

"Louder, Hornick. You're too soft. You have to speak *louder*. You have to be more aggressive."

"I'm trying—"

"Not hard enough."

I roll my eyes. "Yes, Sergeant Instructor Pyle."

Her mouth drops open.

"What did you call me?"

"I . . . um . . . Sergeant Instructor Pyle?"

She gets right into my face, which is kind of hilarious because she's a head shorter than me. The tip of her nose tickles my neck.

"My name is Sergeant Instructor *Spikes*."

"I am so sorry. I must've misheard . . . Sergeant Instructor Spikes."

"Did you just roll your eyes at me, Miss *Thang*?"

"No, no, I didn't—"

"Yes, you did. You have an attitude, Hornick. I know you're in great shape, but just because you're *fit* doesn't mean you're going to last here. Do you understand me?"

"Yes, Sergeant Instructor Pyle. I'm sorry. Sergeant Instructor *Spikes*."

I must have rolled my eyes again because Sergeant Instructor Spikes says, "I got one nerve left and you're leaning on it."

Surprisingly, at the end of those six weeks of Officer Candidates School, I win a leadership award, mainly because I ace every fitness test.

>>>

Back at school for my last year of college, my body is my billboard. Over the summer I've gotten stronger, leaner, and ripped. I like the way I look, and I like that people—men and women— notice me. Many compliment me and ask me to share my workout routine. I tell them the truth: I work out only about forty-five minutes a day.

"You work out for tone," I say. "The key is eating. Seventy-five to eighty percent of this result is from controlling what you eat."

Being so noticed and so identified, I can't let myself slip. I refuse to take a day off from working out and, above all, I remain yoked to my diet.

But when that free day comes around, I fall apart. I lose track of how I eat, I gorge on garbage, and then I feel like crap. I feel overweight, out of control, and down. I certainly wouldn't call Fit Forever a yo-yo diet, but I do seem to bounce up and down from limiting everything I eat, knowing that's keeping me fit, to gorging myself, knowing that's fucking me up. I love that people notice my body. I'm relieved they can't see inside my head.

Senior year I finally live with Kriste. We move into an on-campus apartment with two other girls from the softball team. I also get a job.

I become an instructor at Platoon Fitness, an off-campus gym run by a former Navy SEAL. He puts me through a rigorous fitness test he's designed to weed out the wannabes. I crush the test, and he hires me on the spot. I begin teaching a fitness class three mornings a week outside at the running track of a local high school. I wake up at six o'clock, throw on my workout clothes, and ride my bike to work. Sometimes, if I want an extra workout, I run to and from work, a total distance of four miles. As the months go by and the weather turns cold, I stick to my bike, and even though I wear several pairs of gloves, my hands freeze on the metal of the handlebar.

In the spring of that year, at the midpoint of our season, my dad announces that he is being ordained as a deacon at a Catholic seminary in Wellesley, a town in Greater Boston. I decide to surprise him.

I leave early Saturday morning, change into a dress on the train, and greet my dad at the church. I cry during the ceremony, of course—he does too—and I stay by his side at the reception afterward, his proud daughter. We hang out for a while. I stay overnight at a relative's, and in the morning, before I catch my train back to Philadelphia, he drives me to MIT to see my old high school friend, Becky Clinton, our class valedictorian. Becky and I go for coffee and talk about the future. She has hers planned out like a road map. She has been accepted to medical school and then she will specialize in brain research. I haven't really thought about what I'll do after graduation because I already signed my life away. I will fulfill my military obligation. I will complete my

Marine Corps duty as an officer and serve our country. Beyond that? Go into the FBI or the CIA? I don't know. I love that Becky has found her passion. I hope someday I'll find mine.

As our softball team prepares for a road game against Providence College, I find out that I am receiving a special ROTC award on Friday evening. Coach Q gives me and Kriste permission to accept my award and take a late train that evening to meet up with the team Saturday morning for the game.

My ROTC award inside my duffel bag, Kriste and I pull an all-nighter on the train, talking the whole way, replaying our four years at Villanova, now gone in a flicker—me arriving at college with no more than what I've brought on this train; my first inept attempts at flirting and dating; confronting Coach Q; our series of crazy roommates; working out at dawn; dominating on the softball diamond and winning Big East Pitcher of the Year; and finally living together—many memoires causing us to dissolve into hysterical laughter.

That morning, Kriste and I—giddy and exhausted—emerge into the shocking glare of the train station in Providence, where my dad meets us and delivers us to the stadium in time for warmups. My adrenalin pumping, my body operating on autopilot, my mind a blank, I pitch one of my best games of the season with my dad, the deacon, cheering from the stands. The following week, Kriste and I play our last game as Villanova Wildcats, walk at graduation, and say goodbye to everyone who means something to us, these moments played out in a loop of long hugs, wrenching tears, and booming belly laughs, ending with the two of us swearing to each other, "I promise to always be with you, at your side, no matter what."

9

THE BIG SUCK

2003–2004 / QUANTICO, VIRGINIA

T HE MARINES OFFER ME AN OPTION TO JOIN THE
basic pool of Alpha Company beginning in October instead of signing up with Charlie Company, which starts
right after graduation. The choice to delay my Marine training
for a few months feels like a godsend. Frankly, I'm fried. After
four straight years of busting my butt at school, doing ROTC and
softball—playing something like eighty games a season—I need a
break.

I find a decent apartment and an ideal roommate, a woman
who's never around, and I go to work fulltime at Platoon Fitness.
My plan is to get into absolutely top shape before I start The Basic
School. I consider running the Marine Corps marathon, which
my brothers say is, as marathons go, cake.

In mid-September, six weeks before I officially report to Alpha Company, I arrive in Quantico, Virginia, to join a working platoon consisting of an overlap of Marines from Charlie Company, some of them injured, and incoming soldiers like me from Alpha Company who want to get a head start. I will be sleeping in the barracks and completing daily chores, mostly cleanup, and I will have my evenings and weekends free. With so much time off, I plan to visit Becky, who's in med school at Georgetown.

Pulling onto the base in Quantico, I take in what will be my home for the next seven months—five small nondescript buildings huddled on a wide swatch of flat brown land surrounded by endless, thick woods. As I start to unpack my car, a sudden shiver of cold air stabs through me. I wonder, *If it's this cold now, how cold will it be in those woods when winter comes?*

Cold, I will find out. Really fucking cold.

I share a room with two women, one from Charlie Company who's passing through, the other, Katie Chou, a short, fit, highly intelligent Chinese American who's come out of ROTC at Northwestern with a degree in engineering. We connect immediately, a good thing because we will be roommates from working platoon all the way through The Basic School. Katie oozes confidence and competence. I will gravitate to her whenever I have a question or face a crisis. Katie will save my ass.

The weeks of working platoon feel like a vacation. I work out daily, sometimes with Katie, and train for the marathon, upping my daily runs from five miles to ten, topping out at fifteen miles in the increasingly cool morning mist. I maintain Fit Forever as best I can. At night, we party.

Checking out the few bars in Quantico and determining that they're geared more to locals, we caravan, four or five cars at a time, to bars in Alexandria or Georgetown or D.C., all about forty-five minutes away. I'm no drinker, so I nurse one beer for hours, goofing with the guys in my platoon who are biding their time, waiting, like I am, for The Basic School. I pick up a vibe that a couple of the guys seem interested in me, but I keep my distance. My brothers have warned me that the worst thing I could do is have a romance with a Marine, especially one in my platoon.

"Do not get too chummy with them, Theresa," Paul tells me before I leave for Quantico. "I know these guys. They think of female Marines in three ways: bitches, sluts, or pushovers."

I heed Paul's warning, but it's impossible to stay away from men in the Marines. Besides, I don't see the harm in hanging out, having a few laughs.

In a bar in Alexandria, a real meathead Marine asks me to teach him how to pick up a woman. "I need help," he says. "I don't know how to approach a lady."

"It's not all that hard."

He stares silently into his drink, then lifts his head and says, "Can I do a scenario with you?"

"I guess," I say.

"Great. Okay. So. Here goes." He pauses, then shouts, "HI THERE, BEAUTIFUL! I'M ELMER!"

"Okay, for starters, Elmer," I say, "lower your volume. Bring it way down."

"Copy that."

"Next, lose the 'beautiful.' Ask me my name."

"Roger that. Can we go again?"

"Sure," I say, taking a sip of beer, squashing the urge to laugh.

"Hi there," Elmer says with a smile you'd put on for a dental exam. "I'm Elmer McTeague. What's your name?"

"Theresa."

Elmer, that smile molded on, nods. And nods. And keeps nodding.

"What do you do for a living, Elmer?" I ask.

"I dig holes and shoot guns."

"While that's technically true," I say, breaking character, "you might say instead, 'I'm an officer in the Marine Corps.'"

"Got it," Elmer says.

"Or you could ask me what kind of stuff I like."

"Nice. Okay. Again. Hi, I'm Elmer."

"Theresa."

"Do you like stuff?"

I consider Elmer a work in progress.

>>>

For Alpha Company, Quantico will train six platoons of thirty-three Marines each. My platoon of thirty-three will include two women, Katie Chou and me. A few days before The Basic School officially starts, I receive a visitor: Jen, a woman I met at OCS. She plops down on Katie's cot and makes herself at home.

"I heard you were here," she says. "I wanted to give you a heads-up, see if I can help you in any way.

"That's really . . . thoughtful," I say, unsure about her.

"First, equipment. Definitely get those plastic night glasses, because if you don't have them, you will totally poke your eye out."

"Okay, thank you."

"And be sure to get a gas mask that *fits*. Try it on a lot and make sure it's tight. Because if it doesn't fit, when you get into that gas chamber, you will choke, and your lungs will burn. You do not want that. Now, night land navigation. Very rough. You guys will have it even worse because it'll be winter and freaking cold. You need to be mindful of that and go totally thermal."

"How cold does it get?"

"Okay, I'm not trying to be a bitch, but everyone says you go Charlie Company because Alpha Company freezes their tits off."

"Wow. Must be tough for the guys, too."

"I'm talking about the guys."

Jen laughs, then she leans forward, glances at the door, and lowers her voice. She mentions the name of a woman I know casually. "She is so *dirty*. She's slept with like five different guys."

Jen offers up a smile so snarky I can't tell if she's disgusted or impressed.

She brings up another woman, someone I know only by name. I'd heard she'd gotten married a few weeks before she started The Basic School. According to Jen, in addition to having a husband, she has a boyfriend. I nod dumbly, honestly stunned by all the gossip Jen cheerfully dispenses. She ticks off names as if from a scorecard, listing several more women and all the guys in their company that they're sleeping with.

As Jen talks, I offer a fake smile. I remain stuck in my default mode: polite, courteous, calm. But inside I'm fuming. I can't stand this "who is sleeping with whom" gossip. I feel like I'm back in high school. I want to tell her that we women have to stick together. We struggle constantly to gain the respect of male Marines. They are

our brothers, but they are also our competition. Jen doesn't realize that when she talks trash about these women, she's condemn-
ing them just like the men do. In the Marines, it doesn't matter if
a woman gets involved in a significant relationship or has a steamy
one-night stand. The perception is the same. Her reputation has
been jeopardized.

This double standard angers me. A guy is considered a stud,
his reputation *enhanced*, if he sleeps around or nails a particularly
prized female Marine, especially if she's an officer. A woman is
considered a slut if she sleeps around or beds a prized male Marine. It's unfair and total bullshit and, sadly, the way of the world.
I will encounter this double standard often. I will never accept it.

>>>

The last Sunday of October, along with approximately twenty
thousand other runners, including my dad, who joins me for the last
ten miles, I tough my way through the Marine Corps Marathon.
I've trained well, but I start too fast, blowing through the first half
at a blistering pace, averaging under eight minutes a mile. My dad
has barely trained at all, but he keeps pace with me, and when I
start to fade, he runs by my side, shouting encouragement, even as
we both tire and my legs start to cramp up. As we run, I shout,
"Dad, you don't have to do this. You didn't train."

"It's okay, just one more mile—I'll take it easy," and then
through a time lapse, my brain fuzzy, my legs quivering, we complete the race together. Marines around us applaud and offer us
water bottles and energy bars, and a race official hands me a plastic medal on a lanyard and a t-shirt and gushes that my dad and I
are winners simply because we made it across the finish line.

>>>

I do not, however, rock The Basic School. I do not find The Basic School easy or fun. The Basic School kicks my ass. I find The Basic School to be, as befits its nickname, "The Big Suck."

Right from the jump, our platoon leaders inform us that every Marine Corps officer will be trained as an infantry rifle platoon commander. It does not matter if you end up as a combat engineer, a communications officer, or a financial management specialist. You will know how to lead a platoon. You will be trained to shoot an M16 service rifle and at minimum become a marksman, if not a sharpshooter or expert. You will become intimate with your weapon. Your weapon will become your best friend, your constant companion, your baby. You will *sleep* with your weapon. I adopt a mantra that stays with me from TBS on: *You must become a warrior.*

Before we hit the rifle range, we begin a month of academics.

Coursework. PowerPoints. Instructors droning on in stifling, suffocating classrooms. Within moments of settling at my desk, my eyelids flutter and droop, my eyes close, and I'm out. I doze through important lectures. I wake up lost. To make things worse, we get *homework*. We have to memorize the famous "five-paragraph order," the basis for every strategy in the field, abbreviated as "SMEAC," which stands for Situation, Mission, Execution, Administration and logistics, Command and signal.

I forget what the letters stand for. I struggle to apply the applications correctly when I do remember. I find the logistics confounding at first and then infuriating. I become so frustrated I want to tear the five-paragraph order into a million little pieces and hurl them into the wind.

In class, our instructor assigns us a book to read, *The Art of War* by Sun Tzu, a famous Chinese general and military genius, written in 1772. I find this book so boring, dense, and mystifying that I might as well be reading it in the original Chinese.

I wish I had CliffsNotes. I don't, but I do have my roommate, Katie Chou, who saves me. She soaks up academics like a sponge and helps me understand the key themes and strategies in *The Art of War*. She also guides me as I create semicoherent strategies for my five-paragraph orders so I don't look totally feeble when the instructor calls on me in class.

It turns out I'm not the only one who conks out during classroom instruction. Aside from a couple of military nerds who eat this up like ice cream, the rest of us occasionally doze off. To perk us up, our instructor shows videos of people getting blown up while blasting "Welcome to the Jungle" by Guns N' Roses.

When it comes to physical training, I am an assassin. I work up to twenty pull-ups, no sweat, rip off sit-ups by the hundred, and run three miles in eighteen minutes while carrying a heavy pack. Every morning, Katie and I crank up Liz Phair's "Extraordinary" and drop to the floor of our room. We lock our knees under our cots and crunch one hundred sit-ups, then we squirrel our legs out from under the cots, flip over, and rip off a hundred push-ups. We sweat, we burn, we shout, "*I am extraordinary . . . if you'd ever get to know me. . . .*"

My pulse surging, I put on my game face. I'm scared, but I will not show weakness. I will compete . . . I will *rule* . . . even though I feel as if outside my door I'm running into madness.

We charge out of the room. It's on.

》》》

In December, as the temperature plunges into the twenties and the wind whips raw, we spend a month at the rifle range. We begin at five in the morning by dressing for the entire day and night, then march from our barracks to the range, a mile and a half away. Once at the range, I swap my machine gun for the weapon we're working with that day, either an M16 service rifle or a pistol, and sit on the rock-hard ground, shivering, as a weapons' expert yammers on about shooting technique or safety, encouraging us to take notes. I try to take notes, I try to pay attention, but my hands are numb, my face is so cold my cheeks burn, and the weapons' expert speaks with all the enthusiasm and inflection of a dial tone.

We spend the night at the rifle range. I hand in the M16 service rifle and get back my machine gun. As the temperature dives into the teens and snow starts to fall, I crawl into my sleeping bag and spoon with my gun. The moment I settle in for the night, I have to go to the bathroom. I consider what that entails. I will have to walk half a mile, pull off a dozen layers of clothes, squat in fifteen-degree cold, pull *on* a dozen layers of clothes, and trudge back here, carrying my weapon the whole time.

Screw it. I pee in my pants. At least now I'm warm.

》》》

"Three rounds! Three rounds only!"

I lie on my belly in a row of Marines facing my target, a paper enemy on an easel, a black blotch in the vague outline of a person I picture glowering murderously at me from two hundred yards

83

away. I need to circle this blotch a minimum number of times to become a marksman. I'm going for a head shot.

"Fire when ready!"

I aim. I breathe. I tickle the trigger. I shoot. My shoulder recoils. Around me rifle shots patter like rain hitting a metal roof.

The smoke settles, literally. We rise from our row and approach our targets. We shout our lanes and our numbers and receive our score sheets. I don't have to hear my score. I can see my blotch has only been grazed. I've failed.

I stand, staring at my results, waiting for—I have no idea what. For my numbers to magically improve? For this to be a dream? For me to disappear? As I stand gazing at my score sheet, I become aware that almost all the other Marines have walked away, leaving me and nine others, the only failures. She is a young woman from a different platoon, tall like me, dirty blonde hair, her face all sharp angles and strikingly pretty, her eyes dark brown, almost black and intense, her shoulders surprisingly wide.

"Looks like I have to take this test again," she says, more matter of fact than pissed, her voice deep, the gravelly alto of a former smoker.

"Me too," I say.

"How many chances do we get?"

"One more."

"Or . . . ?"

"Or we have to start TBS all over again," I say.

She roars, almost cackles. "No fucking *way* I'm doing The Big Suck again."

"I hear you," I say, grinning, extending my hand. "I'm Theresa."

She grips it. "Clare."

We retrieve our gear and walk back to the barracks together. From that moment at the rifle range through the rest of TBS, Clare and I stay pretty much joined at the hip.

As with most of my close relationships, we begin with a run, followed by a workout. We run regularly after class, jogging to the weapons building at the farthest end of the compound to work out in its dank gym with creaky floors, threadbare mats, rusted and greasy free weights, the place smelling of sweat and mold. We try to time our workouts so we'll have the gym to ourselves. We don't want to deal with other officers either hassling us or coming on to us.

On our runs, we keep pace and talk, often intimate conversations about our families, struggles, goals in the military and out, and our shared dread that we might fail the weapon qualification test again and be forced to start over at square one. At a weak moment, or perhaps a most trusting moment, I allow myself to confess my deepest concern to Clare. "Sometimes I judge myself so harshly," I say. "I don't feel like an effective leader. How am I supposed to lead when I struggle so much myself?"

"There are all kinds of leaders, Theresa. You're a very charismatic leader. I've heard people say that. You give off this vibe that says anything's possible and everything's going to be all right."

"I don't know, but thank you for saying that."

"It's just a game, Theresa," Clare says. "That's all it is. You were captain of your softball team. It's the same thing. Only with guys. And guns."

"I never thought of it that way."

She's right. I can do this.

The morning of our second—and final—weapons qualification test, Clare and I set ourselves up with our M16 rifles at the two-hundred-yard line. For the past twenty-four hours, I have been visualizing hitting the target dead center as I repeat a mantra, "You're a good Marine, Theresa. Just relax. Stay loose." Now I say aloud to Clare, "We got this. Just remember to breathe," and quietly I close my eyes and pray—*Please let us pass this*—then I open my eyes, sigh, and shoot her a thumbs-up. We take our positions on the ground, wincing as a cold wind cuts through us, dig in, and blast away at our paper targets. When we complete our third round and rush up for our scores, the officer in charge nonchalantly signals that we've both passed, both of us suppressing the urge to scream.

I introduce Clare to Fit Forever, even though in The Basic School, with our nonstop twelve- to fourteen-hour days, I find the diet nearly impossible to maintain. Still I try. My roommate, Katie, and I keep a small refrigerator in our room, which I stock with fruits, vegetables, and healthy snacks I pick up when I drive into town on the weekends. Katie, like most Marines, eats her meals in the chow hall, for me the absolute last resort. When we go on field exercises, the company supplies us with MREs, which stands for "Meals, Ready to Eat"—a box containing a supposedly balanced meal composed of a starter, a main course in a plastic packet, such as meatloaf or beef teriyaki (seriously), crackers, cheese spread, a sticky brown substance resembling peanut butter, and a jiggling green glob that's labeled "dessert." We provide our own definitions for the letters "MRE": "Meals, Rejected by Everyone," "Meals, Rarely Edible," and my favorite, "Meals, Refusing to Excrete." Clare and I pack our own food for field exercises, sharing what we can forage from her fridge and mine, even lugging cans of soup and chili. I always feel on edge, running on empty, and I know I should eat for fuel. But sometimes I don't eat at all.

》》》

In the guts of winter, armed with a map, a compass, and a scorecard, I enter the woods. After mapping out my grid coordinates in the classroom, I begin a two-hour mission to find ten red boxes—out of a hundred—hidden somewhere in the acres of forest, rivers, hills, and valley. The Basic School calls this exercise land navigation.

Easing down a dirt path as an icy wind kicks up, I locate the first box on my map. I count off ten paces. The box should be here. Fastened to a tree. I see no box. I look behind a clump of bare trees. No box. "How many steps do I take for a hundred meters?" I say, frost forming on my cheeks. "Ten, right? Did I overshoot the box? Do I have the right *map*?"

In two hours, I find three boxes.

Clare does no better.

Our platoon commanders assign us to remedial daytime land navigation on Saturday mornings. We enter the woods separately, maps and compasses in hand, counting off paces, occasionally bumping into each other.

"Hey," Clare says, perking up when she sees me. "What's going on?"

"I'm fucking *lost*," I say, not only lost but on the verge of losing it. "I think my compass needle is frozen. Where the hell did I start from? Where's my azimuth? *Where the fuck am I going?*"

"Calm down," Clare says. "Breathe."

"Four stupid boxes. That's all I got."

"You found four? I found two! *Shit*."

Eventually, I locate my ten boxes and graduate to night land navigation.

Even Clare passes night land navigation before I do. I am given one last chance. My platoon commander drives me and five others to our starting points. "See you in two hours," he says.

I check my compass, map, neon nightlight, night goggles, and scorecard, open the door of his jeep, and squint into a freezing rain and a night black as a knockout.

"Shut the fucking door," the platoon commander says.

It takes me an hour to find the first box. Then, running my ass off through the driving rain, I find two more in five minutes.

Three down, seven to go.

The rain lets up and the temperature plummets. I shiver from the cold and from a sudden stabbing fear that I am alone, in the dark, lost, the only sound twigs snapping beneath my boots. I tell myself to be calm, trust my map and my plan. I start climbing up a steep hill. I slip back into a stream of mud. A branch snags my forehead. I curse, check my coordinates, and head into a cluster of trees. There, illuminated by my nightlight, lashed to a metal pole swinging in the wind, I see the fourth red box.

I note my scorecard, consult my map, climb a hill, and find box number five.

And then, negotiating steep inclines on my hands, knees, and stomach, sprinting across clearings, rolling over fallen logs, tripping over tree roots, weaving through mazes of bushes with bristles that tear my clothes and scratch my face, I find the next four boxes.

Takes twenty minutes. Twenty minutes left to find one more box.

I follow my map, surf through a tangle of underbrush, and dash to the bank of a river. Directly across the murky water I see the tenth and final box on a metal pole.

I look at the mouth of the river, at least half a mile away, and I see a bridge. I check the time. Nineteen minutes. I can't make it to the bridge.

I stand on the riverbank, my knees quaking. It starts to hail. I cover my head, ice pellets whapping off my gloves, and step into the river. The freezing water seizes my legs. I howl, and calling up all the strength I've built up in my legs over years of running and weight training, focusing on taking one step at a time, I walk through the river.

The river remains level and only up to my knees, but after five more steps, I lose all feeling in my legs. I grit my teeth and *will* myself to push forward, sloshing through the water, each step slamming my body into what feels like a sheet of ice . . . grunting . . . *shoving* myself forward . . . crashing through the icy muck . . . my body frozen, numb. . . . I slam into the ice water coursing up to my waist . . . toward my final red box.

My foot rises out of the water, and I step onto the riverbank on the other side.

I sink to my knees, yank off my soaked, useless gloves, and check my time.

Twelve minutes to go.

I lift myself off the riverbank and stagger to the red box. I note my scorecard and slide the card into my pack, the hail intensifying, pounding me on the head and neck. I grimace and slide down the muddy bank and back into the river.

The current pulls me. I raise my knee and step forward with as much strength as I can find. My foot lands on a rock and I slip. I go down, slapping the water with my bare hands. I right myself and try to run across the river. Each step I take feels like a knife stabbing my flesh.

Slow down, Theresa.

I do, take one measured step at a time . . . and another . . . and another . . . and finally I step onto the other side of the river.

Six minutes to go.

I look up and face a glistening muddy hill. I run. I reach into a shrub to haul myself up. I grab with both hands and pull—the shrub tears my hands open. Blood spurts. I look closer. I have grabbed a coil of concertina wire. I stare at my hands, split open, blood gushing.

I feel nothing. My hands are so cold that I have lost all sensation. I wipe my bloody palms on my pants, turn toward the road, and try to calculate my pickup point. Through a curtain of thick fog, I can see only a few yards in front of me. I check my time.

Four minutes to go.

I duck into what I believe to be the last cluster of trees before I arrive at the road, a hundred yards away, where my platoon commander waits in his jeep. I take two steps and stop.

Fifty feet ahead, a body hangs from a tree.

My throat swallows a scream. I run in the opposite direction and see another body dangling from a tree. A few feet away, a third body hangs.

Is this some kind of massacre? Should I call this in? Should I cut them down?

I turn and face the first body. My legs carry me closer . . .

In the sliver of moonlight I see that the body is a dummy hanging by a rope. I have walked into the infantry officer training course. I arrive at the dummy and wiggle it, my palms spraying blood. I stare at my hands. Blood covers them, fingertips to wrist.

My watch blinks. Two minutes left.

I lower my head, pump my arms, and run with everything I have. Fifty meters away, the platoon commander's jeep idles. I start to cry. I sprint to the jeep, fling open the door, and collapse on the passenger's seat.

"You made it," the captain says. "Let's see your paper."

My hands shaking, I hand him my scorecard, which looks as if it has been dunked in a bucket of blood.

"What the *fuck*?"

"I split my hands open," I say.

He scans the scorecard. "You passed."

"I did?"

"Yes. Now go get cleaned up."

I gasp, so relieved I cry harder, choking back sob after sob so he won't notice.

>>>

We end The Basic School with urban war games, my favorite training exercise.

We split into five teams, four Marines each, our goal to clear buildings in an urban center, currently a city in Iraq or Afghanistan. Today, the FBI training site serves as Baghdad. Our mission: scout the area, approach a cluster of buildings, enter each structure one by one, hunt for insurgents, engage them, and kill them if necessary. I spend weeks training for this exercise with Elmer McTeague, the meathead Marine who may be a klutz with women but has become an Alpha Company all-star, known as a fighting machine and tactical genius. We work on combat skills, hand-to-hand fighting, and weaponry. "Think *Call to Duty*, only in real life," he says. Some mornings McTeague runs and works out at the gym with Clare and me. When it comes time for urban warfare training, I'm more than prepared. I'm jacked.

Go time. Our team, weapons drawn and loaded with paintball pellets, rushes toward an abandoned two-story building. We fan out at the front entrance. We take our positions. Our team leader signals us and kicks in the door. We enter a wide hallway.

"Stairwell," our team leader whispers.

We check for booby traps. *Clear.* We climb the stairs. *Clear.* We spread out on the second floor, go room to room. *Clear.*

"Go!" our team leader whispers.

We hustle down the staircase, burst through the front door, circle around the back, face a second building, and charge toward that. As we run, machine guns and rifles roar and bullets fly. We hit the ground and return the fire. I get into position and fire my SAW gun, covering my team. They race into the second building. I follow, SAW gun blasting. We flatten ourselves against the walls. The enemy attacks with persistent fire. We're close to getting pinned down.

We return the enemy's fire, but the bullets roar furiously around us. Our team leader crouches, heads toward the back of the building. *BLAM!* He's hit, his back tagged with paint. He falls. A second fire team member falls a few feet away. Then the third member of our fire team stands and takes a chest full of paint. *I'm out of here.* I duck and race down a hallway. With bullets nipping at my heels, I dive headfirst through an open window.

I land on my hand, split open my finger, pick myself up, and *run*.

My finger needs seven stitches, but I'm the only one of my fire team to make it back "alive."

>>>

Each of us writes a wish list for our Military Occupational Specialty (MOS) after TBS graduation, naming five job choices in order of preference. For my top choice, I select public affairs officer, essentially a journalist writing articles, news stories, and press releases, and filming in-house broadcast segments. I put logistics as number two because I can see myself running supplies and equipment needed for missions. I select engineering third because I would get to blow shit up and work at a base in either Hawaii or California; I specify Hawaii. I rank communications and intelligence fourth and fifth. Even though these assignments are highly competitive, my brothers assure me that everybody gets their first or second choice. McTeague gets his first choice, infantry, in Arizona. Katie Chou gets her first choice, logistics, in Hawaii. Clare gets her second choice, intelligence, in Florida.

I get my third choice.

Engineering, in California.

I ask around and get the lowdown on my new platoon, four of whom are among the top-ranked Marines in Alpha Company: a mustang (prior enlisted, older), a former college football player, a total engineering nerd, and a woman who majored in engineering at Rice. And me.

I call my dad and tell him I'll be going into engineering. He sees the posting as a show of confidence and offers encouragement and his prayers. He's reinvented himself, working at a parish in

Scranton, pursuing his new life as a priest. I call Paul next, who goes quiet when I tell him about my engineering MOS, and then I call Bob, now a C-130 pilot and crew leader.

"You're doing engineering?"

"Yeah. I'll be stationed at Camp Pendleton."

"Oh. Good. Great."

Bob says nothing more. The silence lasts so long that I wonder if the line has gone dead.

"Bob?"

"Theresa . . ."

Another long silence.

"You have to be really careful," he says. "Every week I bring a lot of people back in body bags. A lot of . . ." He nearly gags on the next word: "Engineers."

"Okay," I say, dragging the word out to about four syllables.

"They're the ones they put in infantry in recon units. They're needed everywhere. They're in harm's way. They work with EOD techs all the time."

EOD. Explosive Ordinance Disposal.

Bomb squads.

10

TWO BALLS HORNICK

2004 / CAMP LEJEUNE

NESTLED IN NORTHERN NORTH CAROLINA, BOR-
dered by a stretch of sandy beaches, Camp Lejeune almost seems like a seaside town with its golf course, big
box department store, library, movie theater, fitness center,
schools, playgrounds, park, and woodsy area with a stream set off
for hunting and fishing. Our platoon starts each day with physical
training. I rule at this, becoming the de facto fitness team leader.
Here I can tell that the four guys in the squad respect me, even the
mustang and Clinton, the former football player. We've added a
second engineering nerd to the platoon, Mitchell, so now Jeremy,
the original engineer, has a nerd friend.

Our engineering course extends for three months, with three
weeks each devoted to bridge building, construction, demolition,
and obstacle planning. We spend a week locked all day in a classroom

following morning physical training. Our captain, a tall, slim, very laid-back southerner in his midthirties, sometimes joins us for physical training, and when he does, always assigns us the obstacle course. He likes the O course because completing the entire course takes about two minutes. When we're done, I often catch him leaning against the corner of a nearby building, eyes closed, enjoying his morning cigarette.

In the classroom, the captain paces in front of us, lecturing in a languid, deeply narcotic drawl. If I don't fall asleep in the back row—pretty much a given—I force myself to sit in the front row and focus hard. Unfortunately, I find his monotonous voice mesmerizing, but instead of drifting off to sleep, I often fall into a kind of trance. I float away, losing track of time and place. I'm just . . . gone, staring ahead in a daze, as if I've been drugged. One day, as I tumble into this semiconscious state, the captain calls my name.

"Hornick."

"Yes, sir?" I mumble, my filmy eyes trying to home in on him.

"What are you looking at? Do I have a dick growing out of my forehead?"

The laughter around me snaps me fully awake. "No, sir, I don't think so, not that I can see."

We roar louder, all of us, the captain included. He shakes his head and I lower mine, my cheeks burning with embarrassment. But we're all good. Nothing like a belly laugh to bond a squad.

⟫⟫⟫

One day we sit on the lawn, huddled around a staff sergeant who shows us how to determine the density and pH of soil by tasting it.

He digs his grubby fingers into a clump of dirt next to him and dumps the dirt into a mason jar half filled with water. As he mixes the dirt and water with a long spoon, he explains which fruits and vegetables thrive in acidic soil and which prosper in alkaline-based soil. He differentiates various types of soil: sandy, chalky, silty—the soil located near rivers—and clay, normally gooey and sticky.

"What if you're stuck somewhere without a soil testing kit?" the staff sergeant asks gravely. "You need to rely on your knowledge and ingenuity."

He takes a moment, sniffs the soil in the jar, swirls the soil-water mixture like it's a fine wine, and then he *drinks* it. He swishes the dirt in his mouth, swallows, frowns, and says, "Subtle, a little salty, no acidity at all. Definitely alkaline." He then passes the jar of dirt around for us to taste. When the jar comes to me, I take a small sip, nearly gag on what smells like compost, chase it with a chug from my water bottle, and wonder, *Is this on the Fit Forever plan, or do I have to wait and eat dirt on my free day?*

After we each sip the soil cocktail, the staff sergeant mutters something about being able to test the density of soil by adding a certain chemical, a drop of which he plops from a vial he produces from the back pocket of his cammies into another glass jar filled with dirt. I watch him pour the chemical into the jar of dirt, and then . . .

My eyes start to close. I fight the urge to fade away, I'm not going to sleep . . . I'm going to fight this off. . . .

I lose.

I don't know how long I take this little nap, but I miss the staff sergeant dropping two small steel balls into the second jar of dirt.

When I jerk awake, I see the staff sergeant violently shaking the jar of dirt, and I hear the steel balls clanging. Of course, I know nothing about any steel balls.

"Wow," I say to Clinton, the football player, who sits next to me. "That is some loud soil."

"Huh?"

"Why the hell is it so loud? That's incredible."

"What are you talking about?"

I stare at Clinton. He is so *thick*. "You can't hear that? The soil is *clanging*."

He opens his mouth, closes it, opens it again.

"Clinton," I say patiently. "That noise you hear is because of the *chemical* he put in there. Didn't you see him do that? It must've made the soil hard or something."

A part choking, part high-pitched caw—a noise I've not heard come out of a human before—blows out of Clinton's mouth. Then Clinton starts to honk like a goose. He's *laughing*.

Now everyone starts to lose it.

The staff sergeant nods, looks at me, and then dumps the soil mix onto the ground. The two balls roll out.

"Whoa," I say, amazed. "It's a magic trick. How did you do that?"

"Hornick," the captain says. "Didn't you see him put the two balls into the jar?"

"The two . . . ? Oh. Yes. Okay. No. I did not."

"Two Balls," Clinton says.

"Yeah," I say, feeling like a total fool. "I realize that now. He put two steel balls into the jar."

"No," Clinton says. "From now on, that's your *name*. Two Balls. Two Balls Hornick."

It sticks.

〉〉〉

We train in martial arts.

We meet every other day for an hour, learn fighting techniques, then smack the crap out of each other. I love it.

Donnie, a friend of my brother's, a black belt recon Marine—special forces that operate behind enemy lines—is our instructor. Donnie likes to hit. He especially loves opening up his "toolkit," an assortment of poles, sticks, and padded bayonets, and wailing on us with his weapon of choice for the day. He seems particularly partial to sticks.

Maybe because I'm a woman and someone he knows and he refuses to cut me any slack, he goes harder on me than anyone else. He thrashes me. At first, I'm not sure how to respond.

"Come at me, Theresa!"

I attack him at half speed. Donnie dances out of the way, blocks my half-assed blow, and slams me on the side of the head.

That pisses me off. I bull-rush him.

"That's it!" Donnie shouts. "Come on!"

He deflects my stick, spins, and whacks me again, this time on the back of the thigh. My leg buckles. I can already feel a welt reddening and rising.

Now I'm really pissed. I back up, move toward him, fake right. Donnie goes for the fake. I go left, whirl the stick almost as if I'm delivering a fastball, and slam him in the stomach.

He grunts, folds, kneels, the breath knocked out of him. He holds up his hand like a stop sign. He blows out some air.

I relax.

Donnie swings from his heels, hits me so hard I leave my feet. I land on my ass. "Never drop your guard," he says, out of breath. He reaches his hand to help me up. I swat his arm away with my stick. He gets to his feet, comes at me. I pirouette away and slap him on the side of the face. He looks shocked, then he grins. "People! Do not mess with her. Seriously." He faces the rest of the platoon. "We got us a *warrior*."

>>>

We learn to build bridges, jersey barriers, vehicle checkpoints, and cement obstacles, then we learn to blow them up. Led by a staff sergeant explosives expert, we march into the barren hills above Camp Lejeune. As we sit on the rocky ground, our rifles cradled into our shoulders, the staff sergeant demonstrates the use of plastic explosives, dynamite, and menacing fifteen-pound steel charges that look like miniature missile heads. This guy, a jittery, shaved-head pyrotechnics geek, speaks in run-on sentences and a low monotone, as if he's sat too close to too many explosions.

"You face the charge upright and then, whoosh, as it hurtles down, the explosive turns the cone into a hot, molten steel slug that can blast through pretty much anything, an armored vehicle, a tank, a bridge, talking here a very powerful explosive."

The staff sergeant musters us to our feet, and we arrange a series of metal stands at ten-foot intervals. We carefully set the fifteen-pound charges into each stand and lock them all down.

I retreat several meters back. Something about handling hot explosives capable of blowing up a freaking *bridge* makes me feel squirmy and unsettled. I scrunch my forehead and try to grasp the barrage of terms and instructions flying at me—*blasting cap, three points of contact, crimping* ("Crimp!" "Yes sir!"), *fuse, canister,* all followed by the staff sergeant's frantic directives, "Bury that!" "Push it in a quarter turn," and "Twist it, don't pull it!"

We blast away at the hillside with our explosives, dynamite, and murderous steel charges, protecting ourselves in bunkers, as chunks of dirt, rock, and uprooted plants rain on us. We watch how to lay a land mine and learn how to go pyro, a protocol used to scatter approaching civilians or potential insurgents by screaming, warning, and, if necessary, shooting the ground around them, even setting off a land mine or exploding a charge if people refuse to disperse.

It all seems surreal and vaguely fun for a while, as if we're kids playing war. But then something changes in me, maybe in all of us, and a kind of darkness sets in—call it reality—bringing with it weight, gravity, and deadly seriousness, and I feel a sense of urgency . . . and, if I allow myself to go there, the slightest dry-mouthed taste of fear.

11

A FEW GOOD WOMEN

2004–2005 / CAMP PENDLETON, CALIFORNIA

T HE WEEKEND AFTER I GRADUATE FROM ENGINEER-
ing school, I fly to Albany, New York, to attend my
brother Bob's wedding. Big Bob is marrying Lisa—sweet,
kind, slightly shy, and very pretty.

We've been talking about Bob's wedding for months. My dad,
only a year away from being ordained as a priest, will perform the
ceremony. I will be a bridesmaid and read a passage that Bob and
Lisa have chosen. Paul, too, has promised to participate. "I am
gonna *party*," he says.

The family convenes in the lobby of the hotel in Albany like
Marines swarming a beach. My dad and I check into our room;
we're sharing a large room nearly the size of a suite. I choose my
bed, the one nearer the window, and while Dad pores over his

notes, I go into the bathroom and try on my purple bridesmaid's dress, size eight.

I close the door, grit my teeth, and start to wriggle into the dress. Whoa. Shit. *Shit.*

I knew the dress would be tight—I should be wearing a size ten—but I didn't expect to have to *squeeze* into the thing. Finally, sucking down gobs of air, I wrestle the dress on. I look in the mirror. Okay, I have to admit, I look pretty. I can't really *move*, but we all know that with beauty comes pain.

Bob's wedding is beautiful. I read my passage; Dad marries him and Lisa; Dad cries; I cry; I try not to do a header off my stiletto heels or fall out of my too-tight purple bridesmaid's dress; we all stand, applaud, and cheer as Bob and Lisa enter the reception hall; we all dance; and then we take our seats for dinner. The food comes . . . and comes . . . and keeps coming. I eat it all. I can't stop myself. I don't even know what I'm eating. I don't care. If it lands in front of me, I eat it.

I do more than overeat. I make myself ill.

Later, illuminated by a spotlight in the center of the dance floor, the bride and groom shove chunks of cake into each other's faces, and in their honor, I feed myself a fistful of cake, licking the icing. Soon after, Bob and Lisa prepare to leave, and I hug them goodbye, then, shoes off, I stagger into the elevator, lurch down the hall to my hotel room, unlock the door, and collapse onto my bed, feeling drunk on food, sick on food, disgusted by food, beaten up by food, every moment—joyful or stressful—a trigger. For twenty-four hours, I feel hung over, even though I didn't take a sip of alcohol. When I finally find my equilibrium, I don't want to look at food. I don't want to look at food ever again.

>>>

With six weeks to go before I report to Camp Pendleton and take charge of my engineering combat platoon, I load up my temperamental Nissan Xterra and drive from Camp Lejeune in North Carolina to Ohio to become a fitness queen.

Before entering The Basic School, I had heard about a world-renowned bodybuilder-nutritionist-fitness-guru, Philip, who offered private coaching Monday through Friday at his house in a Cleveland suburb. I call him, and Philip gives me his pitch. He will work me out, get me in shape for photo spreads and fitness competitions, adjust my diet to make me even leaner, and put me up and feed me, all for the unbelievably low price of $1,000. I decide to give myself a present for graduating from engineering school. I sign up for Philip's intensive five-day session.

I pull into a circular driveway that fronts a large two-story colonial in an expensive suburban tract. I press the doorbell, and Philip, lean and muscular, greets me with his wife—or girlfriend, I never do get their relationship straight—a woman named Madeline, a former Miss Olympia, who poses in the doorframe, her entire body as tan and taut as a leather belt. They escort me to my quarters, a spacious guest room just down the hall from their master bedroom suite.

In the room, which smells of vanilla incense, a gift basket awaits me on the nightstand. I pull apart the silver cellophane wrapping and find a bound notebook containing a schedule of workout times, mealtimes, and snack times; a diet plan; rules of the house printed in a large, bold font; samples of supplements I can purchase through Philip's company; an assortment of energy bars, pills, and protein powders; and a paperback copy of Madeline's self-published autobiography.

The next morning I meet Philip and Madeline on their wide back lawn for a brisk thirty-minute warm-up, after which we convene in their country kitchen for breakfast—a protein shake blended with egg whites. We then pile into Philip's van, and to grating New Age music pumped through bass-heavy speakers, we go to his private gym in a nearby mall and weight train for three hours. Each day we concentrate on a specific part of the body—arms one day, legs the next, then torso and chest, back to arms, ending with legs. All morning, a steady stream of bodybuilders flows through the facility, men and women, all flamboyantly dressed in hot-pink or neon-green short shorts or leotards, all full of energy and obsessed with themselves, constantly preening in the ubiquitous mirrors along every wall.

At night the three of us eat a dinner cooked by Madeline, a tiny portion of chicken or fish accompanied by two meager asparagus stalks or three puny broccoli florets. During the day, Philip allows me two snacks, a late-morning protein shake and a midafternoon energy bar. Soon after dinner, I retire to bed. I manage a few pages of Madeline's memoir, which chronicles her battle with anorexia, then by nine o'clock I crash, exhausted. By Wednesday night, I'm famished. Thursday night, I can't take it anymore. Every iota of discipline I felt has gone.

I roll out of bed around eleven, ease the door open and tiptoe into the kitchen. I fling open the refrigerator and find a platter of chicken, already cooked, skinless and glistening, obviously Friday night's dinner. I grab a meaty thigh and start gnawing on it.

"Are you supposed to be eating that?"

Madeline. In the doorway. Glaring at me.

"Oh, my God," I say, through a mouthful of delicious chicken. "I'm so hungry."

"We have rules," she says.

"I know. I'm sorry. I'm just . . . *starving.*"

"Well." She literally sticks her nose in the air. "I made exactly sixteen ounces for tomorrow. Make sure you don't eat your portion tonight."

I don't give a shit, I think.

"I'm really sorry," I say. "I'm so embarrassed."

The next morning, Philip and I go alone to the gym. We don't speak until we pull into a parking spot at the mall.

"You have to really want this," Philip says. "It's a very serious business, a twenty-four-hour commitment, all day every day."

"Okay," I say, both of us knowing that I lack the chops or devotion or, frankly, narcissism, required to make it in the world of professional bodybuilding and fitness modeling. Even so, I don't quit.

❯❯❯

On my way out of town, I stop at a health food store and pack my cooler with food for the road, taking care to avoid anything that contains white flour, salt, or sugar. I head west, my destination Sacramento, California, where I will spend a week with Paul, who has become a personal trainer after completing his duty with the Marines. He offers to work out with me in preparation for a fitness competition I'm thinking of entering in October in Anaheim, although if I'm honest, after my week in Ohio I have lost the fire for it. Still, I remain committed to staying in shape and eating right—and, I can't lie, to looking good.

I drive long stretches at a time, stopping only to use roadside rest stops and to exercise. When I start to feel antsy or drowsy, I pull over to the side of the road, not caring if I'm on a country road or an interstate highway. I get out of the Nissan and go into a ten-minute exercise routine—jumping jacks, push-ups, and squats. As I work out next to my idling SUV, horns honk and assholes hoot. I don't care. I need to keep the blood flowing so my muscles won't atrophy and I won't fall asleep at the wheel.

As for meals, I don't eat them. I guzzle water and snack on bananas, eggs, energy bars, and packets of dry instant oatmeal, cinnamon flavor, my favorite. As I drive, I tear open individual packets and pour the oatmeal into my mouth, chasing it with gulps of water.

In Sacramento, my brother Paul puts me up in his spare bedroom, and we set up a training routine. We run twice a day, logging long distances and sprinting murderous intervals around a local high school track. We work our legs, hamstrings, quads, and calves, then we do sets of squats to tighten our butts. Over the weekend we drive up to San Francisco to hang with Paul's on-again, off-again, high-maintenance girlfriend, Vicki, a model and multiple beauty pageant winner who will be running the Nike half-marathon in the city. We gather in her apartment the day before the race. Vicki, five four, super trim, super tight, wearing a freshly painted golden tan, the proud owner of brand-new torpedo-shaped, extra pointy boobs, flashes a pair of theater tickets at me—two box seats to see Liz Phair.

After the concert, in the cab on the way back to her apartment, Vicki leans over and pinches my leg. "You are getting really lean, Theresa. I hear you may enter that pageant in Anaheim."

"Thinking about it."

"It's a good one. I won it a couple of years ago."

"Paul told me," I say.

"I've been in beauty pageants my whole life, since I was a little kid," Vicki says, peering out her window into darkness, light from streetlamps slicing her face. "My mom put so much pressure on me. You have no idea." She looks down at her breasts and shakes her head. "So fake, huh?"

"Well," I say. "I mean, you can't really tell—"

"*So* fake," Vicki says. "I felt I had to get them to stand out. Give me an edge." She frowns at her breasts. "I always have to win. It's horrible."

"I can relate to that," I say, but Vicki's looking off into the night again, and I don't think she hears me.

"The key is, you have to control your food." Vicki nods at her reflection in the window. "I throw up when I eat. I have a problem."

She turns away from her reflection and looks at me.

"Sometimes I'll eat an entire pie with ice cream, then I'll feel awful and I'll make myself throw up. Then in the morning I'll eat a bowl of oatmeal, feel bloated, and throw up again. Tomorrow, before the race, I'll throw up. I don't want all that food in my stomach. It weighs me down."

I have no idea what to say. She seems so vulnerable and so sad. I'm surprised that she's sharing this with me and I think, *Why would you do that?*

And then as if to answer me, Vicki says, "It's easy. I don't even think about it."

I feel so sorry for you, I think.

"Theresa," Vicki says, looking at me as if she's privy to a secret about me that I don't know myself. "It's so easy."

I spend a few more days with Paul in Sacramento, then I pack up and prepare to drive south to Camp Pendleton to pick up my platoon. I will live off base in Poway, about forty-five minutes away, with my new sister-in-law, Lisa, while Bob is deployed. As I load up my wounded Nissan, now in severe need of service—the car's been wheezing since Reno—Paul heaves my go bag into the way back. "I'm really stoked that you have a platoon, Theresa," he says. "It's awesome that you'll be working with engineering guys."

"I hear a large *but* coming."

"You're their leader, not their friend. I don't want you to get eaten up like a lot of women do in the Marines."

"Not gonna happen. Trust me."

"I do," Paul says. "And remember, if you want their respect—"

"Run their dicks into the dirt."

He smiles. We hug. I hit the road.

▶▶▶

Lisa lives in a small one-bedroom apartment with a loft and a private bathroom, my living quarters until I get my own place closer to the base or I get deployed. I arrive at her place on a Saturday afternoon, two days before I report to Camp Pendleton to take over my platoon. As I turn onto her street, the Nissan starts to cough. I pull into her driveway, and the car dies.

"I don't know what I'm gonna do," I say to Lisa, after I unpack the Nissan and settle into my bedroom. "I have to leave Monday morning for Camp Pendleton and I don't have a car."

"Take Bob's truck," Lisa says. "He'd be honored."

Monday morning, I wake at 0500, shower, press my uniform, buff my second lieutenant's bars, and take a final check of myself in the mirror. I leave Lisa's apartment at 0600 in the cool and the dark and settle behind the wheel of Bob's big-ass shiny fire-engine-red Ford F-150 with Marine Corps license plates. I slip Guns N' Roses into Bob's souped-up sound system, his fleet of subwoofers rumbling the bass line so hard the truck shakes as I turn up the street.

Forty-five minutes later, emerging through a dense brown fog, I approach the main gates at Camp Pendleton, 125,000 acres of military compound, hills and forests bordering one side, the Pacific coastline on the other. Once I pass through the gates, I cut off the CD, slow Bob's rig to fifteen miles an hour, and drive another twenty minutes across the base to reach my platoon. As I pull into my parking space, a cluster of idling Marines parts, their eyes glued on this ridiculously massive red vehicle, all of them no doubt wondering—worrying—what kind of badass Marine *is* this new lieutenant?

I step down from Bob's truck and smile.

Your badass lieutenant is a woman.

I meet the company's commanding officer, the XO—thirties, dour, snub-nosed, slope-shouldered, and cold—who reveals his true colors when he screams at his pregnant Marine assistant to get him coffee. Later I say hello to the other platoon commander, also new, a woman I remember from Officer Candidates School. My captain puts in a cameo appearance, flashing me a wide, insincere smile.

Then the screen door flies open, and Timothy Hall, my gunnery sergeant, blows in. Think Kevin Hart in the Marines.

Sergeant Hall snaps off a salute, sizes me up, and slowly shakes his head. "I'm gonna have to crane my neck up to you," he says, doing just that. "Wow. You're tall, ma'am."

"I'm the shortest in my family," I say.

"I'm the tallest in mine," he says, holds, and we both laugh. He then lowers his voice. "Can we talk?"

Before I can answer, Sergeant Hall streaks to the far end of the office and drags two chairs into a corner. He waits for me to sit. When I do, he edges his chair close and leans in. "Ma'am, I want you to know, I'm gonna keep you going. Everything in this platoon goes through me. Everything. I'm gonna make sure you're very well informed. Always in the loop. That's a given because I *own* the loop. I *am* the damn loop. I'll make sure you look good. That's my mission."

"Back at you," I say. "We'll make sure we both look good."

"I hear that. Loud as a bugle in my ear. All right," Sergeant Hall says, standing up, kicking back his chair. He looks up at me again. "Man, ma'am. You must work out. Do you?"

"On occasion."

"I expect it's more than on occasion."

"You're about to find out."

He grins. "That's what I was afraid of, given my own somewhat erratic exercise schedule. So. I expect you'll want to say hello to the platoon?"

"I would." I check my watch. "In an hour?"

"Yes, ma'am. We'll gather at the parade deck. That work?"

"Sounds good."

"Okay, then if I'm excused, I need to talk to the other platoon's gunny. Gonna tell him I won."

"You won?"

"Absolutely." Sergeant Hall winks. "My ma'am can definitely beat up his ma'am."

》》》

I stand in front of my platoon, fifty Marines, most of them eighteen or nineteen years old, only two of them women. I want to make them feel comfortable and I want to motivate them. I want to prepare them for war.

"How you all doing? I'm Lieutenant Hornick. I'm originally from Seattle. I will want you all to get into great shape. And I want you to be prepared. But preparation goes both ways. I can teach you and train you, but I know I'll also learn from you. I want us to help each other. I also want to get to know you individually. So, in the new few days, I'm going to reach out to each of you. And if you ever have any questions, please ask me. I'm always available to you. Now, tomorrow is our first PT session, at 0700. I look forward to seeing what you got. Any questions right now? No? See you tomorrow, bright and early."

I search their faces for signs of how they feel. They seem motivated.

And scared shitless.

I begin our first PT session, Paul's words ringing in my head. *Run their dicks into the dirt.*

First I lead calisthenics, and then I lead a charge behind the engineering support battalion up a hill known as Heart Attack Hill. I run, head down, outpacing everyone, shocking these nineteen-year-old guys, watching them drop back one by one, gasping, massaging their sides, their faces flushed. At one point, I slow to a jog, allowing everyone to regroup and catch up. Huffing, my gunny pulls up next to me.

"Ma'am, if I may?" He holds up his hand, more to give himself a moment to catch his breath than to ask my permission to speak. "Ma'am, please, you have *got* to slow down. You're losing every-body. Plus . . ." He waves his hand again. "I smoke. I am a smoker. I think I may die. Right here, right now. So, it's been a real plea-sure—"

"Okay, point taken," I say. "I'll slow down."

"A wise decision, I promise you." He pauses. "You don't have a cigarette on you, do you? I left mine at the chow hall."

We laugh so loud the Marines jerk their heads in our direction.

>>>

Hurry up and wait.

First week in my platoon I see a lot of that, minus the hurry. I see my Marines hanging around, sitting around, goofing around, wasting time. Doing nothing.

I vow to change that.

I want my platoon in shape, mentally and physically, for when we deploy. Because I know—we all know—that inevitably we *will* be deployed.

And so I work them.

I train them hard, my PT sessions becoming legendary, ac-cording to my gunny. "*Legendary*" is one word I hear. I also hear "*feared*," "*dreaded*," and my favorite, "*torture*." I don't mind be-cause I can see my Marines getting fitter right before my eyes; I see their bodies changing—less flab, more muscle. Their running times improve. Their endurance increases. They become stronger, and with this strength comes more confidence. I notice too that several of my Marines start putting in extra time at the gym, at lunch or during free time. I continue to run their dicks into the dirt. I lead them on ten-mile hikes, full packs on, up and down hills, through woods and rough terrain in the rain, and when it gets hot, tromping across sand, maybe the most strenuous of all.

We do convoy training, we work demolition and land navigation, and we build obstacles and blow them up. We spend hours at the rifle range. We work on martial arts. I divide the platoon into fire teams, and we practice urban warfare. I add a classroom element and some book study, and I keep my platoon on top of current events, which we discuss in small groups. When we can, we meet outside so nobody falls asleep. I share everything I've learned, and I learn as much as I share.

>>>

Urged on by Vicki, Paul's girlfriend, who volunteers to be my coach during a persuasive phone call, I enter the fitness competition in Anaheim, called Model America. I check the calendar. I have six weeks to get into runway shape. Not a problem, Coach Vicki assures me. Even though I no longer feel the passion I once had for modeling and fitness pageants, I'm turned on by the idea of becoming leaner, of training, of pushing myself.

I work all day, completing last-minute paperwork, waiting until my last Marine has gone for the day, sometimes as late as seven o'clock, then I hit the gym. I crush the elliptical machine and then go through a punishing speed workout with heavy weights. Every night in the gym, I feel the Marines who work out with me gawking. One officer I know comes over to me after I finish a set of squats and says, "Damn, Theresa, I would love to have legs like yours."

I also watch my food. I remember Vicki's key to winning fitness competitions: control what you eat. I take her literally. I eat almost nothing.

Most nights, I pull into Lisa's driveway in Poway around nine-thirty and stagger up to my room, totally spent. I go straight to bed, eating almost nothing for hours, my stomach burning from hunger.

The week before the fitness competition, a few days before she and Paul are to arrive, Vicki calls me for a last-minute coaching session. "First," she says, "and this is extremely important, you must have a serious tan."

"I don't have a lot of time to lie on the beach," I tell her.

"A *fake* tan, Theresa. Spray it on. Gobs of it. Lacquer yourself up. Do not hold back. Spray until you look like Beyonce."

"Okay . . ."

"Now, swimsuit. Where we at?"

I describe what I'm wearing.

Vicki groans. "No, Theresa, oh *no*."

"It's hot pink," I say.

Silence. I can hear the former beauty queen's mind whirring. "Okay, look, honey, I'm coming down there tomorrow. We're going to La Jolla to one of those cute boutique bikini shops, and we're buying something flashy."

"Vicki," I say. "I *work*. I'm in charge of fifty-three Marines. I can't take time off to go bikini shopping."

"Fine, I get it. I'm still coming early. Now, what about your creative outfit? What do we have going there?"

"It's actually fun. I'm wearing my softball helmet, a cutoff softball t-shirt, short shorts, high socks and heels. I'm going to wear my glove and carry a baseball bat on my shoulder."

"Hilarious," Vicki says. "Theresa, we're gonna win this thing."

We give it our best shot.

I snazzy up my bikini by sewing sequins all over it. I find a purple evening dress at the Exchange on the base. I buy it a size too small so I have to squeeze into it, making sure it comes off looking semislinky and I come across looking curvaceous. Vicki arrives early and gives me a lesson in walking in high heels. She supervises my spray tanning. She also coaches me on how to walk across the stage sexily, stressing that I have to flirt with the judges, which I refuse to do.

Backstage at the Anaheim Convention Center, with my small but rabid fan base camped in the front row—Vicki, Paul, Lisa, and Kelly, my former roommate at Villanova who has flown in from Philly for the occasion—I sit in front of a makeup mirror, staring at my smudged reflection, elbowed continuously by tanning-cream-heavy, hairspray-spritzing, fake-boob-lugging, five-foot-six-inch, one-hundred-twenty-pound, bleached-blonde twigs grappling over hot irons, hair curlers, and eyebrow pencils, feeling as if I'm some Amazon extra from *Land of the Giants* who has wandered into the wrong dressing room. And yet . . . I suddenly want this. I want to win. I've logged so many extra hours at the gym, run so many additional torturous miles, worked out so hard, and *starved* myself and . . . *I want to win.*

And I know I won't. I know I can't. I'm too tall. Too out of place. Too different. I hear my name. Climbing to my feet and teetering on my high heels despite Vicki's expert coaching, I clop onto the stage, trying to maintain my composure and keep my posture erect as I squint into the blinding footlights, Vicki and Kelly clapping and screaming from the front row and Paul barking, "Ooh-rah, Theresa . . . Marine Corps!" and I want to holler at the judges, "Look at my ass all you want, you lechers, you have no idea who I am!"

Afterward, we all go to the Cheesecake Factory, and I eat so much I want to throw up. I can't stand feeling so full and so sick. I glance across the table at Vicki, who has put on weight since I last saw her in San Francisco, and I can tell by the look she shoots back at me that she knows exactly what I'm thinking. Later she and Paul leave, and Kelly tells me about her job at an accounting firm while I tell her about being a Marine.

"You're thin," she says. "You look good. How are you feeling?"

I shrug, because at that moment I really don't know.

"I feel . . . a lot," I say.

"Do you worry about being sent to Iraq?"

"I try not to think about it. I just do my job. I lead my platoon. If I get called over there, so be it. It's my duty. I want to serve." I hold for a moment. "I know that all sounds canned, but it's not."

"I know it's not," Kelly says. "You're the most genuine person I know."

>>>

On Monday at 0700, I run PT with a vengeance. After what amounts to a three-mile sprint up Heart Attack Hill, my gunny, Sergeant Hall, pulls up, bends over, coughs, gags, spits, and mumbles, "I'm down to two cigs a day. About to have my first."

"You ought to quit altogether," I say.

"I know that." He grimaces, rubs the back of his leg.

"You all right?"

"I'm great. Except for my hammies. And my ass. After training with you, I couldn't sit on the toilet for a week. That was a compliment." He groans and stretches to his full height. He looks at me and frowns. "If I may say, ma'am, you are so tan."

"I know. I just did a fitness competition."

"You're very dark. We could be twins."

>>>

I want to keep thin. I want to keep tight. I want to use the competition that I lost as motivation. I want to keep training overtime and stick to eating miniscule meals of almost exclusively protein.

But I can't. My body rebels. I take an unplanned hiatus from training after my work day because my body won't let me push myself.

And I crave food. A constant hunger shoots through me like electricity. I start to binge. I begin one night after Lisa has turned in, earplugs and night mask on, dead to the world. I pad down the stairs of my loft into the kitchen and raid the refrigerator and pantry.

I gorge myself on whatever box of sugary cereal I can find, then I weave back upstairs, throw myself on my bed, and feeling fat and filthy, judging myself, revolted at the thought that I may be gaining weight, I lie curled up in the covers until the sugar swamps me like a wave and knocks me out.

I sneak downstairs night after night, binge, totter back upstairs, fall into bed, and wait for the sugar wave to wallop me until I pass out.

And then one night I do it. Downstairs, I ransack the refrigerator, find nothing appealing, start rummaging through the shelves of the pantry, and grab a box of Cinnamon Toast Crunch cereal. I rip open the cardboard top, shove my hand inside the box, and shovel the sweet dry squares of cereal into my mouth. I scoop out a second handful. Then a third. Soon I eat the entire box of cereal, dry, my cheeks puffed out like a bear.

Within seconds, I feel gross. Disgusting. Dirty. Like a fat fucking pig. I know what I'm going to do. What I have to do. But before I do it, I actually have a conversation with myself. *I am going to do it just this one time, because I will not be eating like this anymore, ever again.*

I run upstairs to my bathroom and throw up. I feel better instantly. I feel . . . free.

Later, lying in bed, my hand resting on my stomach, my head throbbing with guilt, I say, *Why did you do that? That was fucked up. Never do that again.*

I don't do it again. For two more days.

I crave everything sugary and fatty. Designated the apartment's food shopper, I load up on snacks and boxes of cereal I know Lisa will like too. Then every night I wait until I'm sure she's asleep, and I tiptoe into the kitchen and raid the pantry. I continue the conversation in my head, desperately trying to convince myself to stop sneaking around like I'm having an affair, my lovers sexy Cinnamon Toast Crunch and hunky Golden Grahams. After every illicit late-night liaison, I swear that this will be the last time, so help me.

I eat and eat and eat until I feel spacey and bloated, then I feel pissed off and gross and repulsed. To empty myself of these feelings, to try to gain some control over all I have eaten, I throw up . . . twice a week.

One night, Lisa catches me with my arm up to the elbow in a box of cereal. I feel myself flush as she stares at me, her face contorted in confusion.

"You eat at night a lot, don't you?" she asks.

"Yeah," I say. "I'm so hungry. My whole family. We're big eaters. We eat all the time. We're always hungry."

She smiles unconvincingly and backs away, retreating to her bedroom. I wait, then I devour the rest of the box of cereal. Almost immediately, I feel angry and bloated and full of regret. And sick. Physically sick. Mentally sick. My mind bounces from thought to thought . . . I feel depressed . . . I feel sad . . . I feel anxious, fat, disgusting . . . and then I throw up.

After being busted by Lisa, I decide to curtail my late-night binging at the apartment, so I stop at fast food places after work. I stop at Arby's, Wendy's, Taco Bell, Carl's Jr., Jack in the Box, Burger King, and McDonald's. I lust for them all and their beef tacos, chicken patty melts, and my favorite, burgers, two or three at a time, Hoovering up fistfuls of bun and burger slathered with sauce, cheese, mustard, mayonnaise, ketchup—the greasier the better, eating right off the soggy burger paper crinkling in my lap as I drive to Poway. By the time I turn into Lisa's driveway, I feel so disgusted, light-headed, and listless that I rush into the bathroom the moment I walk in the door.

>>>

After the fitness competition, I decide not to let all my training and starving myself go to waste, and I hire someone to build a website. I'm still interested in pursuing a fitness modeling career, and I see the website as my portfolio and my résumé. I design the website to include training tips, a fitness blog that I write, and photos from some of my competitions, including one of me in a swimsuit, as well as a shot of Paul and me standing in front of the American flag. Nothing salacious. Nothing controversial. Everything done in good taste.

The XO goes ballistic. He calls me into his office and, looking even more dour than usual, steers me to his desk. His laptop sits open to my website, the picture of me in my swimsuit facing us both.

"Why would you want to do this?" he asks, slapping his desk. "Do you know how unprofessional this is?"

"Well, respectfully, sir, I disagree. I think it's very tasteful. I'm a fitness model." On his laptop, I scroll through a few of the photos in my website gallery. "Look. That's my brother."

"I don't care who it is. I find it appalling. The Marines are young and impressionable, and they could get the wrong idea. They could look at you *differently*. They could . . ."—he swallows before he speaks—"act out."

"Act out?"

"*Yes*," he shouts.

"I'm sorry, sir, I don't understand the problem. You see the same photos in fitness magazines, volleyball magazines. Worse. These are much tamer. I would like to continue to get work as a fitness model, maybe motivate people, especially young women. This is my résumé."

"You need to do something about this website."

"Are you ordering me to take it down?"

"I can't order you to take it down. But I can strongly suggest it.

Which I am. Use your judgment. You're a platoon commander. Do your job. So you decide."

"There are no lives at stake here," I say. "It's just a couple of harmless pictures."

He straightens up as tall as his slope shoulders will take him. "Your call."

I opt not to take my website down.

I make the wrong call.

》》》

"Do you know him to be worthy?" The voice echoes through the cathedral.

A forceful baritone answers. "Yes. I know Joseph Hornick to be worthy."

Sitting in the first row behind my dad, who sits on the altar before the bishop, both men draped in white robes, I feel the tears seeping down my cheeks.

We gather, our family, extended family, and close friends, in the sanctuary of Saint Peter's Cathedral in Scranton, Pennsylvania, witnesses to my father's ordination, the culmination ceremony of his becoming a Catholic priest. The bishop leans slightly forward and speaks to my father about embracing a life rooted in prayer, reiterating his priestly obligations—presenting the Eucharist, hearing confession, and offering counseling.

Later, as my father lies prostrate on the altar and the bishop rises and lays his hand on him, completing the rite of ordination, I dab at my cheeks. Filled with love and pride for my dad, I try in vain to fight off the one urgent thought that sears into me right now—*Father, I need to confess and I seek your counsel.*

Afterward, we eat. We convene at a barbecue on the church grounds, greasy ribs and fried chicken piled high on buffet tables, food that so recently I would hungrily throw down and then instantly throw up, food that at this minute I avoid. I summon a reservoir of resistance, feeling desperately alone even though I'm with my family, fighting the urge to eat, knowing that if I take one piece of chicken, I won't be able to stop. I feel my arms quiver, my hands shake. I cruise the buffet table, reaching the desserts, pies, cakes, cookies, and at the end, the devil, a cheesecake that I fixate on, a creamy, tantalizing cheesecake, taunting me, daring me . . . and I think . . . *I'm afraid of the cheesecake.*

I spend the weekend sharing a hotel room with my dad. I leave the barbecue early, go to the room, and write in the journal I've been keeping, scribbling random thoughts and feelings, my words overwrought, emotional, and disconnected. I feel better when I write, even if what I write makes little sense.

When my dad comes in for the night, we talk about the ordination, and I tell him how happy I am for him, especially that he has found something he loves, a path that suits him perfectly. Exhausted, he gets into his bed and turns out the light. I take a deep breath. I decide to confess and seek his counsel. "Dad, I've been struggling with . . . eating . . . a little bit."

"Struggling how?"

"Sometimes I throw up."

After a long beat, he says, "Do you know why you're doing that?"

"I don't know. I try to eat healthy, and when I don't, I throw up. It's not only that. I have a lot of stress. It's the extremes. I can be feeling very down or very up. It doesn't matter. High or low, either one can be a trigger. Sometimes I want to take a break, to disappear into some quiet invisible space, but I know I can't, I have to be on alert . . ."

I hear a low rumble.

"Dad?"

He rumbles louder.

I realize then that he has fallen asleep.

〉〉〉

When I return to Camp Pendleton, I receive two new bits of information. First, we will be leaving for a month-long mountain warfare training exercise in the mountains near Bridgeport, California.

Second, Sergeant Hall informs me that he's moving to a different platoon in our unit, the one led by the other woman platoon commander.

"Feels like they're breaking up a good team," I say.

"No doubt," he says. "But we'll bump into each other, I promise, especially up in Bridgeport. And you'll be good with your new staff sergeant. He'll like working with you, I know that. Everybody likes working with you, ma'am."

"Not everybody."

Sergeant Hall shouts out a laugh. "Seriously, ma'am, don't let the XO get you down. You're doing all the right stuff. You got plenty of support. Just stay the path, straight and true. You'll be all right."

"I appreciate that."

"I enjoyed working with you, sincerely."

"It was a pleasure, Sergeant Hall. I'm going to miss you."

"Back at you," he says.

My new gunny, Staff Sergeant Rigsbey, brings with him a reputation for sarcasm and in-your-face honesty.

"I'm gonna tell you right now," he says when we meet, "I have not worked with a woman. This will be new to me."

"We're all Marines here, Sergeant Rigsbey. Just Marines. Your job is to keep our particular group of Marines in line. Kick some ass, if you have to."

He grins. "I like you already."

I get along famously with Sergeant Rigsbey.

>>>

We bus to Bridgeport, the Marine Corps mountain warfare training site, miles of snowy mountain hills with trails winding through walls of jagged rocks rising to an elevation of ten thousand feet. I live in a female-only barracks, the four enlisted Marines sharing one room, the other platoon commander and me sharing bunk beds in an adjacent room.

The first morning we gather in a classroom for a lesson in cold-weather survival. The subject: food. I drift toward the back of the room and lean against the wall, as a stocky survivor guide with thick, hooded eyebrows and a disturbing smile walks to a metal laboratory sink in front of the class. He cradles a live rabbit against his chest.

"So, you have no food, you're alone, and you must survive," the guide says, standing at the sink, his dark, hooded eyes darting around the class. "Here's one thing you can do."

He puts the rabbit into the sink, breaks its neck with his bare hands, pulls a knife, and skins it.

As the rabbit bleeds out, I look away for a moment, then I turn back and lock into the survivor guide, who begins to list all the parts of the rabbit that are good enough to eat. "Of course, do not forget the most delicious part," he says. "The eyeballs."

The room goes silent.

Because we all know what he is about to do.

"You find yourself stranded in the snow? You need to avoid getting dehydrated. Rabbit eyes. An excellent source of electrolytes."

He squeezes the rabbit's head, pops out one of the eyeballs, and eats it.

"Now," the guide barks. "Who wants the other eyeball?"

"Lieutenant Hornick!" someone shouts.

"Go for it!"

"YEAH!"

Shouting. Applause.

It takes me a few seconds to realize that the entire roomful of Marines is facing me.

My forehead pulses hot.

Well, okay.

Guess I have to eat that eyeball now.

Shoulders back, I muscle past a trio of Marines and walk to the front of the classroom, the Marines chanting at my back, "*Lieutenant Hornick, Hornick, Hornick . . .*"

I face the survivor guide and hold out my hand.

His smile fades, his eyes narrow to black slits, and then he squeezes the dead rabbit's head, yanks out the eyeball, and drops it into my palm.

I pop the eyeball into my mouth.

The Marines go wild.

I chew the rabbit's eyeball and I swallow it.

The Marines cheer.

I walk back to my spot at the back of the classroom, slapping palms and bumping fists on the way.

His lesson complete, the guide moves aside, replaced by another officer who will explain how to light our propane stove in below-zero temperatures. I don't hear a word this officer says because I've tuned out. And then, pretending to fight a sudden wave of fatigue, I yawn, spit the eyeball into my hand and stick it into my pocket.

"Ma'am?"

Survivor guide.

I blink.

"I saw you put the eyeball in your pocket," he whispers.

I shift my position against the wall.

"Busted," I say.

"Nah. You're cool. This'll be our secret. But . . ."

"Yeah?"

"Can I have it?"

I reach into my pocket and hand him the eyeball.

"Enjoy," I say.

He licks his lips, and then he eats it.

>>>

At a bar one night, I run into a couple of Marine officers I know from The Basic School. We order drinks and share stories from Lejeune and Pendleton and other places we've been posted. By the second or third drink—I nurse one beer, order another, and feel guilty as hell about that—we get rowdy and funny and personal. One guy brings up a Marine I know, Rene, who, rumor has it, gets around.

"I thought she was the love of my life," the Marine says. "I thought she felt the same. Then I found out she was sleeping with this total yoo-hoo the same time she was sleeping with me."

"What a whore," the other Marine says.

"Now, see," I say, wagging my finger at him, "if Rene was a guy, you'd be calling him a stud."

"Dude," the first Marine says to me. "I'm trying to tell you. I loved her. I would've gotten serious with her. Maybe gone the distance. She broke my heart. I lost all respect for her."

"Why? Because she wasn't serious about *you*?" I say. "Sounds like she just wanted to have fun."

"I think Two Balls has a point," the second Marine says.

"We call it a double standard," I say. "Ever hear of that?"

"No," the first Marine says, signaling the bartender for another round.

After finishing our drinks, we head to their barracks for a nightcap, and the two Marines bring up The Basic School.

"You were the PT queen," the first Marine says to me. "You kicked *ass*."

"Not really. TBS kicked my ass."

The second Marine suddenly starts laughing. "We all heard about your safety briefs."

"They weren't that funny."

"Heard they were *hilarious*," the first Marine says.

"Do one," the second Marine says.

"No," I say.

"Please," the first Marine says.

"*No*," I say, then I suddenly stand at attention and stare at both Marines. "All right, listen *up*."

I pause and then raise my voice.

"First off, don't be an idiot and drink and drive. If I ever hear of you drinking and driving, I will seriously cock-punch you. Instead of drinking, drink a gallon of water, go to the beach, play volleyball, work out, and go for a run. Drinking sucks. You wake up feeling like shit. You know why that sucks? First thing in the morning, you have to be ready for my physical training session at *0700*. And if either of you puke or drop out, your ass is mine. Now. Safe sex. Respect each other. And don't be an idiot. Wear a condom. Instead of having sex, drink a gallon of water, go to the beach, play volleyball, work out, and go for a run. Sex sucks. You wake up in the morning feeling like shit . . ."

By now both Marines are on the floor, convulsing with laughter. And then I lose it too.

⫸⫸⫸

The XO calls me into his office. He wastes no time busting my ass.

"Heard you had quite a little party last night."

"I'm sorry?"

"You and a couple other officers were seen at the bar, drinking, getting rowdy, and then you all left together. You want to explain yourself?"

"Those guys are friends of mine from TBS. We were just hanging out."

"In their barracks?"

I hold, feeling outrage bubbling. "We weren't doing anything."

"That doesn't matter. It looks bad. Very unprofessional. You're a Marine officer. You're up here on a training mission. This is not high school."

"Sir—"

"I don't want to hear it. We're done here."

After that, I make myself three promises.

I promise to perform at my highest level, be on my best behavior, and win over my XO.

I go two for three.

>>>

We continue our field exercises, two or more a week, each one more demanding, difficult, and miserable than the one before. We increase the load in our packs, carrying sixty, seventy-five, a hundred pounds on our backs. We go on longer and longer hikes—eight miles, ten, twelve—staying in tents in subzero temperatures for four nights in a row. We blow up the side of a snowy mountain with explosives, creating an avalanche, our mission to read the falling snow, ice, and rock so we can avoid getting buried alive in the landslide.

We receive instructions for our last training exercise, a four-mile night hike, in which I will lead three platoons, more than one hundred Marines, from point A to point B. The exercise simulates combat conditions, and I must create the safest, most efficient route to our destination. I plot a route along a river, easy to follow, no way to get lost, safer in my opinion, but admittedly longer and more challenging than taking the conventional inland road.

Right from the start, I encounter a problem.

The river route provides no trail, and many of the Marines simply can't handle the rough terrain and steep incline of the river-bank. A shocking number of Marines fall back, drifting off on their own. Only a few can keep up with me. The slower the Marines move, the later it gets, the colder the night. I constantly stop the march to allow the Marines to catch up and to permit the staff sergeants to maintain something resembling a formation. I feel as if they're herding cats. And then my walkie-talkie bleats.

"You need to stop and wait!" The XO.

He has joined our exercise, taken a position at the rear. I swear I can hear him wheezing through the tinny speaker of my walkie-talkie, trying to catch his breath.

"Sir, respectfully, I can't wait too long. I don't want people to get hypothermia."

"You're going too *fast*."

I want to say, *I'm not going too fast. These Marines just can't keep up with me*, but I don't go there.

When my staff sergeant gives me the word that we're ready to continue, I move. Slightly slower. Still too fast for the Marines and the XO.

"Lieutenant Hornick! Stop! You need to wait longer."

I hold up, and as the few of us in the lead wait for the others to reach us, I start to see signs of hypothermia in a few of the Marines—shivering, dull, drowsy eyes, and one Marine's lips have turned a sickly blue.

"Sir," I say into the walkie-talkie. "We seriously cannot wait. People are starting to struggle with hypothermia. We have to move on. Doesn't matter if we move at a slow pace, but we have to move!"

"Goddamnit, Lieutenant Hornick! Fuck this. Get up on the road!"

I can't argue with him. He outranks me. I feel disciplined and humiliated. But mostly I feel that I have failed.

I lead the Marines to the road. As we go, I see that the Marine whose lips have turned blue can barely walk. I put my arm around his shoulders and support him as he walks uncertainly, assuring him that he's going to be fine. At the same time, I signal my gunny to radio for an ambulance. When we arrive at the road, the ambulance is waiting. I lead the Marine toward two EMTs, who ease him onto a gurney.

Shortly, the rest of the Marines join us on the road. I start to move toward the front, but I'm stopped in my tracks by a roar at my back. "You have no idea what the fuck you're doing!"

I turn and face the XO. Raging, he waves the walkie-talkie at the sky. "You needed to stop."

"We needed to *go*," I say, low, gesturing at the EMTs sliding the stricken Marine into the ambulance. "I knew that if we didn't keep moving, something like this was gonna happen."

"I could've told you that these Marines couldn't go that route. But you didn't ask. You like to do everything on your own, don't you? You hate asking for help."

"I have no problem asking for help."

"You do," the XO says evenly, angrily. "And that will be your downfall."

》》》

A day after the botched training mission, I sit by myself in the chow hall, fiddling with a salt shaker, feeling depressed, homesick, and dizzy. I have fought to keep food down and have for the most part failed. I have recently looked at a calendar and counted the days until we return to Camp Pendleton and I get to spend a few days over Christmas with my family. I desperately need a break.

I lower my head and close my eyes, and then I sense a presence. The table wobbles as a guy sits down across from me. I recognize him. Short, muscular, thinning hair, flashing a smile that takes you in. A staff sergeant from the other lieutenant's platoon.

"That hot mess the other night?" he says. "Wasn't your fault."

I sigh and prepare to push away from the table. I'm not in the mood to talk about this right now.

"Fucking Marines are supposed to be tough," he says. "That's why we're Marines and not the volunteer fire department or the Coast Guard, right?"

I actually laugh. "You would think."

"Not always the case. As we saw."

"I, for one, believe in conditioning."

"So I've heard." He extends his hand. "Adam Lauritzen."

I shake his hand. Firm grip. Something genuine in his eyes.

"That was a training exercise," he says. "That's all it was, an exercise. Things go wrong. People make mistakes. That's the point. That's how you learn. By the way, I think you were right going along the river."

"I appreciate what you're saying. It was still messed up. And when you're the officer in charge, you take responsibility. At least I do. So when things go wrong, it's on me."

He leans back in his chair. "You're different. You got a quality I don't see a lot. You care. You actually want your Marines to succeed."

I don't say anything.

"What you did with that Marine who got hypothermia? How you stood up to the XO, who's an all-pro douche bag? I want to work with you."

I press my fingers into the table. "I feel like this is a job interview. So, Adam Lauritzen, tell me about yourself and why I should hire you."

He laughs, then he does tell me about himself. Almost the first thing he says is that his dad passed away when he was very young and his single mom raised him. I tell him about my mom's passing and my dad's raising me. We're struck by how much we have in common. We talk for an hour, Marines swirling around us, the clatter of utensils scraping plates, loud voices, laughter, none of it distracting us, all dissolving into a dim background hum.

Adam and I talk about loss, how much he misses his dad and I miss my mom, how we dealt with being *that kid*, the one deemed different, an outcast, simply because we didn't come from a conventional two-parent family. We talk about his close relationship with his mom and mine with my dad. We talk about fitting in here, in the Marines, struggling to find a place, admitting that sometimes our biggest challenge is staying true to ourselves. By the time we end our conversation, the first we'll have of many, I've snapped out of my funk, knowing that I have made a rare connection and a friend for life.

❯❯❯

Over Christmas the whole family—Dad, Bob, who is back from Iraq, Lisa, and Paul, solo—rolls into Poway for the holiday. I'm hoping for a quiet, uneventful Christmas eve at Lisa's, but I get a call that a Marine in my platoon has received a DUI. At midnight, I drive to the base and spend over an hour filling out paperwork and familiarizing myself with the appropriate punishment to hand out to the Marine—severe, it turns out, but not career ending.

We spend Christmas day at a restaurant known for its sumptuous buffet. Numb from the night before at the base, I linger by the fruit bowl at the far corner of the buffet, debating whether to ladle a few blueberries onto my plate and call it a day or eat a pile of pancakes and puke later. My dad eases up next to me, pretends to agonize over which type of melon he wants, and then says, as casually as he can, "How you doing?"

"Okay," I say. "Been better, been worse."

He peers at my plate. "You're not eating much."

"Not that hungry right now."

"Are you still having . . . issues?"

"Yes."

"Okay . . ."

"I'm . . ." I look away, feeling a sudden catch in my throat, then I turn back to him. "I'm trying," I say.

"Good," my dad says. "That's good."

I decide to go for the pancakes.

Twenty minutes later, I excuse myself from our table and throw up in the ladies' room.

Later, my brother Paul decides to walk off his meal and asks me to join him. We walk up Lisa's block, our heads down, eyes on the sidewalk, our pace slow.

"Are you okay?" Paul finally asks.

"I'm fine."

"You seem off. Sort of anxious."

"I'm just distracted. Thinking about being sent to Iraq or Afghanistan, don't know when, could be any day. I guess I'm a little on edge."

"You should read this book I just finished, *How to Stop Worrying and Start Living*. Do you good."

"Yeah?"

"Yeah. You worry a lot."

I rake my fingers through my hair. "Maybe I do. I'll read it."

"I'm buying it for you." He holds for a moment. "The key is to prepare. Worrying won't help. Stressing out won't help. Prepare yourself as much as you can."

"I will," I say. "Thanks."

We keep walking. I slip my hand into the fold of my brother's arm.

12

I'M DYING TODAY

JANUARY—FEBRUARY 2005 / LAREDO, TEXAS

WITH MY BROTHER BOB HOME FOR GOOD, I MOVE into a house close to Camp Pendleton with two other women: a logistics officer and a good friend, Dr. Martin, the medical officer in charge of our entire battalion. I couldn't ask for better digs. I have a large bedroom, my own bathroom, and a small office area that I turn into an exercise room with a few free weights and an exercise bicycle, a gift from my dad. Each morning before I head off to work, I spend forty-five minutes riding the bike and watching the news, showering, eating sugar-coated dry cereal or oatmeal out of the box, and then throwing up. I chalk it up to stress. We live in limbo. We know we will be deployed. We just don't know when or where.

We get the word. We're going to Iraq. Fallujah.

First, though, to get accustomed to a climate with oppressive heat and to help the border patrol halt the flow of illegals from Mexico, we head to Laredo, Texas, for eight weeks to build a twelve-foot-high cast-iron fence, a road, and a bridge. Before we go, the CO overseeing the entire operation and I meet with the engineer who has designed the construction. The engineer patiently walks us through a baffling set of blueprints. I admit that I'm out of my league. The CO compliments me on my honesty, and the engineer supplies me with a CliffsNotes version of the plans in plain English—my own personal cheat sheet, which I break down later into a daily to-do list. After the meeting, the CO, a fortyish, old-school Marine, asks me to hold up.

"Lieutenant Hornick, I just want to say that you're doing great. I love your passion. You're a good leader."

"Thank you, sir."

"That's all. Enjoy Laredo."

"Oh, you won't be going?"

"No, but you'll be well looked after."

He sends my favorite XO.

>>>

Our battalion of about two hundred Marines takes over an old Army reserve base on a bleak strip of parched dirt along the Rio Grande, just across from Mexico. The base faces a Mexican prison from which we routinely view explosions of smoke and fire and hear gunshots and screams.

I am in charge of seventy Marines, sixty-nine of them men. I have my own room and bathroom down the hall from the XO, a new CO who outranks him—a scarecrow of a guy on his first deployment—and two other officers, one a friend from Camp Lejeune and the other a corpsman, a high-level medic who stands about six five, wears his hair gelled and stylish, and lathers himself in cologne.

We first bulldoze the area and then we dig holes four feet deep, in which we insert enormous concrete fence posts. I designate the work, allowing Adam, now my staff sergeant, to first outline and then oversee the day's tasks. I don't believe in micromanaging. I firmly believe that undermines my Marines' motivation and strips them of any feeling of accomplishment. The new CO doesn't agree. He seems to spend his entire day peering over my shoulder, keeping a watchful eye on the progress of the project. Either he feels personally responsible for the success of this fence or he doesn't trust me. Maybe both. In any case, he's somewhere between a nag and a well-meaning pain in my ass. In the course of a typical day, my walkie-talkie squawks ten times an hour with complaints from the CO, such as "Lieutenant Hornick, I have a Marine here literally *sleeping* on the job. Get over here."

Not sure which I prefer: dealing with this new niggling micromanager or the jackass XO who spends his days skulking around the job site like a ghoulish building inspector trolling for mistakes, once screaming at me that a few yards of fencing had been installed improperly, tearing it out, and stomping on it, his face pulsing purple. Tough call.

I assign four Marines a simple job: take a company truck to the equipment site, load up the truck with five cast-iron fence posts, and drive the posts to the building site. Factoring in ten minutes for loading the posts and another five minutes for fucking around, I estimate the job should take no more than twenty minutes, round trip.

The Marines disappear for two hours.

The CO frantically screams into my walkie-talkie, "Where the hell is that truck?"

"I don't know. They had strict instructions—"

"Get to the bottom of this. And Lieutenant, this is on you."

When I get to the building site, I find Rigsbey standing next to the truck with the four Marines, none of them yet twenty-one, all looking stricken.

"What the *fuck*?" I say, climbing out of my Jeep. I notice then that the right rear tire of the truck sits bunched around its rim. "What happened here? Where the hell are the fence posts?"

Rigsbey shoots a death stare at the four Marines, who shuffle in front of him, their eyes down, studying the dirt.

"They never got to the equipment site," Rigsbey says. "They took the truck on a little joy ride instead."

"I don't even want to know," I say.

"They blew out that rear tire and drove back here on the rim."

"Nice," I say, catching a roll of the eyes from Rigsbey. I roll my eyes in solidarity.

I walk over to them, go from guy to guy. I'm taller than each of them. "So, you guys want to play around? Okay. I'll play. From now on, the rest of today, tomorrow, and every day, you will *carry* the fence posts to the job site. You will not use a truck. You lost that privilege. You will never use a truck again. And you still have to get the job done in the same amount of time. Now get to work and get out of my sight."

I slam my fists against my hips. The four Marines remain standing by the truck, still shifting their weight, still studying the dirt.

"What are you guys waiting for?" Rigsbey says. "You heard the lieutenant. Move your asses. Go get those fence posts."

The shortest, heaviest Marine mumbles something and starts slouching toward the building site. The others shuffle slowly behind him.

"Gee-*zus*," Rigsbey says. "You guys are pathetic. What a bunch of little fuck-ups. How about you walk in cadence! Move it!"

He calls a cadence, just as my walkie-talkie trills. It's the CO, in a snit. "So? Where are we with that truck?"

I start to explain, but Rigsbey screams, *"What?"* at the heavyset Marine, getting into his face and drowning me out. Later, with the four guys' silhouettes hauling the cast-iron fence posts in the distance, Rigsbey arrives at my Jeep as I'm guzzling a bottle of water, his face one big sheepish grin. "Well, you did a really good job with them. They called you the c-word."

"They what?"

"Yep. Congratulations. They hate you. That means you have officially become a leader."

I burn. I can barely look at him.

"I want to see everyone—every single Marine in my platoon—before dinner."

"Yes, ma'am," Rigsbey says.

Standing in front of forty Marines, my hands locked behind my back, I begin to speak, my voice quavering at first, then rising with a power I did not know I possessed.

"I want you men—because you are all men, except for one of you, and right now I am not talking to her—I want you to consider what you have here. It's Laredo. It's hot. It's boring. That's too bad. Boo-fucking-hoo. You have three squares a day, a roof over your heads, and spending money in your pockets. You get to be with your buddies, but people, this all comes with a price. It's not free. You also have to do a little *work*. You have a job to do. You've got to build this fence. You signed up for this. You signed up to serve your country. You are Marines."

I pause. Look them over.

"Marines," I repeat. "The best of the best. That's what I think. That's what I believe. Do you believe that? Do you think you are the best of the best? *Do* you?"

A roar of "*Yes, ma'am*," led by Rigsbey.

"Oh, you *do*?"

Now I floor it.

"Well, that's odd, because today we had a few Marines call me the c-word."

Silence.

"That's right. These guys called me a *cunt*."

I pace in front of them, feeling my face warming and my voice rising.

"I got to say, that word? Calling me that? That hurt me. I have bent over backwards to help you guys. I don't micromanage you. I don't get in your face. I let you manage yourselves. Because I believe in you. I believe in you because you're Marines."

I hold. "I'm sorry. I *believed* in you. Past tense. I don't believe in you anymore. I can't. I can't respect you because by calling me that name, the worst name you can possibly call a woman, you obviously don't respect *me*. Would you call your sister a cunt? Your girlfriend? Your wife? Your mother? Would you?"

Now I lose it. I build to a scream.

"I guess I have to change. I guess if you're going to call me a cunt, I might as well *be* a cunt. But you know what I think? If I'm a cunt, you're a bunch of pussies. All of you. A bunch of fucking pussies. So here's how it's gonna go from now on. I will be a cunt. When I say jump, you fucking bitches better jump. When I say walk, you fucking pussies will walk. When I say work, you ass-holes *work*. When I say play—*if* I say play—you little fucking cocksuckers play. And if I ever hear you call me anything derogatory again, you will be doing PT with me at five o'clock every morning so I make sure you work a thirteen-hour day, you dick-less pieces of shit. Yeah. Dickless pieces of shit. Which makes you . . . guess what . . . *cunts*. You're all fucking cunts, every one of you. You sicken me."

I turn to leave, then wheel on them, my face on fire.

"You know what? I changed my mind. Tomorrow morning. PT. Five A.M. O-five-hundred. I want to see all your asses outside. I'm gonna run you little bitches into the ground and then you can go work your thirteen-hour day, and you little fuck-up pussy cunts can build your FUCKING FENCE!"

I storm out.

"Damn," Rigsbey says to me later, after I have calmed myself somewhat by throwing up. "I guess I'm wearing the skirt now. You really put the hammer down."

"Yeah, well, they fucking deserved it."

"And I think they needed it."

Almost on cue, three Marines approach tentatively. One, apparently the preappointed spokesperson, steps forward. "Ma'am, I just want you to know that we would never call you a cunt."

"Never," the second member of the trio says.

"Very disrespectful," the third Marine says.

"Uncalled for," the first Marine says.

"Thanks," I say. "Now spread the word. Tell your colleagues that."

"Yes, ma'am," the first Marine says. "And thank you again for your speech. It was very motivating."

The rest of the evening, Marines seek me out to apologize on behalf of their disrespectful colleagues and to swear that they themselves would never call me the c-word, ever, under any circumstances. Before I turn in for the night, the CO congratulates me; the sleazy corpsman gushes a bunch of mindless bullshit, his cologne causing my eyes to tear; and the XO, typically, goes MIA and doesn't seek me out at all.

After that speech, I feel a shift. I feel as if the men see me as a leader. I spoke a language they understood—their language—and they responded. At least for now. I know it won't last, but that doesn't matter. Of course, they recognize that I am a woman. But now they know that I'm not a pushover, that I won't take any shit.

They called me a cunt and I grew some balls.

>>>

I cry every night. I feel alone and hungry and ugly and weak, whiplashed from mood to mood, from being caught in the depths of some deep, dark pit to feeling as wired as a coke fiend. Every free moment I have, I work out, alone, at the base's decrepit gym. Every morning, I run the perimeter of the base, alone, imagining that I'm running through the outskirts of hell. During meals, I devour MREs, hating every bite, fighting every morsel, and then

I sneak away and throw up, twice a day, three times, four. At night, I mentally scratch off the days like a prisoner in solitary, and then I sob myself to sleep. This is all temporary, I tell myself. It's this place. This place crushes you. I hear the mournful song. I hear Johnny Cash's gritty voice.

> *As I walked out on the streets of Laredo.*
> *. . . The hot sun was setting . . .*
> *I know I must die.*

I'm one jagged nerve ending, sizzling in this heat, in no mood to fuck around or be fucked with, determined to complete this job, pushing my Marines to build this fence on time. We have only a couple of weeks left here, thankfully, and other than work, a barbecue on the last weekend, and a company softball game Adam has organized, we have nothing on the docket.

I'm looking forward to the softball game. Adam has been begging me to pitch. At first I backed off, feeling too much pressure because of my reputation, but then the XO, in a blatant in-my-face challenge, told Adam that he can't wait to bat against me. Adam reported that the XO said something like, "Maybe she can pitch okay for a woman—you know, that underhand shit—but I played *baseball*."

Yes, I am looking forward to that softball game.

⟫⟫⟫

Meanwhile, sitting on a towel draped over a box of supplies in the baking heat, the creepy corpsman pulls a box over and sits down next to me. We don't say anything for a while, and other than the coconut cologne that wafts over me, I forget he's even there until he says, "So, listen, I just want to say, I really enjoy talking with you."

"Huh? Oh, yeah, me too. I enjoy talking to you." I spring up and shout to one of my clumsy Marines who's heading in the wrong direction with a coil of fencing, "Hey, Bowzer, where you going with that? It's *fencing*. It folds right in with the other *fencing*. Because, see, you're making a *fence*. Thank you." I slump back onto the box.

"You're great," the corpsman says, laughing. "I just *love* talking to you. So, listen, I'm on the rear party leaving a week after everyone, staying extra time to wrap things up, and I was thinking it would be really awesome if you could arrange to be on the rear party too."

I squint at him. "Why?"

"It might be fun."

"Fun? What are you talking about? Look around. It's like we landed on the surface of the sun."

Another shotgun laugh, then he says, "Look, you're nice, I'm nice, and there's no use hiding it, we have a certain obvious . . . connection. So you get on the rear party, we could hang out. You could come over to my room, we could unwind from all this, maybe give each other a nice, slow massage—"

I blink so furiously he must think dust flew into my eye. I stammer and spurt, "What the *fuck*? Like, you went from, I really enjoy talking with you to me giving you a massage in your room?"

"Yeah, I kind of thought—"

It's the heat, my moodiness, my light-headedness, my anxiety, and it's also him, this creep, all of it, and I shoot off the box of supplies and get into his face, as close as I can without gagging on his cologne, and I explode. "You nasty ugly-ass piece of shit. You're married. You have kids. Aside from that, I would never, ever, in this lifetime, if we were the only two people left alive, come within ten feet of you."

"Look, okay, calm down, I only thought—"

"You don't *think*. You assume. And you grope. You're a disgusting, inappropriate, harassing asshole, and if you ever speak to me again . . . if you come within a hundred yards of me . . . I. Will. Fuck. You. Up."

He stands. He's three inches taller than me, but I don't back off.

"Is that a threat?"

"No," I say. "Not at all. When I finish for the day, I'm calling Dr. Martin, your boss, who, as it turns out, is my *roommate*, and I'm reporting you. That's not a threat at all. That's a fucking promise."

I kick over the box of supplies and move away. We avoid communicating that day and for the rest of our time in Laredo.

I call Dr. Martin after work and drop the hammer. The corpsman receives a written warning, a slap on the wrist. Eventually, I hear through the grapevine that he comes on to another Marine, who turns him in, and he receives a severe penalty—hopefully a punch in the mouth instead of a slap on the wrist.

⟫⟫⟫

We create a baseball diamond in the dirt, laying down flak jackets for bases, and we divide into teams. Adam catches for our team, and I pitch, windmilling fastball after fastball, mixing in an occasional drop ball or curve just to mess these guys up. Every Marine I face either flails helplessly at my fastball or stands frozen, barely able to see the pitch before it smacks into Adam's mitt. No one can touch me. Good. Because I'm in no mood.

Then the XO strides to the plate, digs in, waggling the bat, a bat I brought from home, and points off like he's Babe Fucking Ruth.

Man, this guy's an arrogant prick.

I whip my arm around and throw a fastball high and tight, an inch away from his chin, bending him backward.

"Sorry," I say. "It slipped."

His face darkens. "Throw me one where I can hit it," he says. "Or are you afraid of me?"

"Yeah," I say, "that's it."

I gun a fastball right down the middle. He looks at it. He can't move.

"Try this one," I say. Another fastball. Right down the middle. Again he freezes.

He stares at me. "Now, is this any way to treat your mentor?"

My . . . *mentor?* Is he delusional?

I grit my teeth and go into my usual whipsaw motion. Only this time I pull the string.

I throw him a breaking ball that heads straight for the center of the plate, but just as the XO begins to swing, the ball drops like it's rolling off a table. In the middle of his violent swing, he cork-screws himself into the ground and falls flat on his ass.

"I believe that would be strike three," I say.

Adam helps him up.

"You win," he says, shooting me a high beam of stink eye. "This time."

At last we leave Laredo and return to Pendleton for a couple more months of prep before we go to Iraq. I spend the last few days organizing our departure, tying up loose ends, and trying to get a grip on my life. Those are the words I use, the prayer I whisper every night after I throw up, before I cry myself to sleep: *Please, Theresa, get a grip.*

I'm losing it.

I'm losing control.

13

CALL TO DUTY

2005 / CAMP PENDLETON

O N A COLD, GRIMY DAY, I LIE BEHIND A SHRUB IN the hills above Camp Pendleton, learning the "nine-line," the proper procedure to guide pilots from choppers and harrier jets so they can medevac wounded soldiers out of enemy territory. I scour the crusty meadow below with binoculars, scanning for the crucial information I need to scribble on each of the nine lines on the crinkled sheet of paper at my side. If I make an error, I could put the pilots and my wounded colleagues in mortal danger. Certain I've gotten all nine lines down correctly, I scramble to my feet. The captain in charge of the exercise calls on me first. "Okay, Lieutenant, what does this line do?"

I answer, reel off the next four lines, reach line six, and stumble.

"Ambulatory or litter?" the captain asks. *Walking wounded or needing a stretcher?*

"Ambulatory," I say. "I think."

"No hesitation," he says. "Do it again."

I move to the side of the small supply hut.

"You'll get it."

I look up and see a captain I recognize from another unit, a harrier pilot doing a mandatory ground tour. He's tall, stocky, with a surprising paunch—not into working out, I can tell that—and he's older, which you can see by his graying sideburns. I'm not sure if I find him attractive, but he does have kind eyes, and I like the way he smiles.

"I'm Chase," he says, offering me his hand.

I shake his hand. A little fishy. Guess we can work on that.

He asks me to dinner. I agree, after first examining my no-dating-a-Marine policy. I don't see him on a daily basis—he's doing a ground tour on the other side of the base—and he's not in my unit. So he qualifies. And honestly, I'm only vaguely attracted to him.

At dinner we click. He seems sensitive, genuinely interested in me and my story, and unlike most guys, he *listens*. He too grew up with a single parent, his mom, and understands my close relationship with my dad. He likes that I'm an athlete and wants me to meet his friend Monica, a well-known beach volleyball player. He offers to fly us all to Vegas for a weekend. We linger over dinner, talking and laughing, but as we hunker down at our table, grazing through our appetizers, gobbling our mains and sides, sharing a dessert, my anxiety builds, and even though I smile broadly at Chase, all I really care about is when I can get home and throw up.

We set up a date to fly to Vegas. I ask Chase if I can bring a friend, and I invite Katie Chou, my roommate from TBS, who's in from Hawaii visiting family in San Diego for a few days. I'm not sure how I really feel about Chase, and I value her opinion. To ensure we arrive at the airstrip on time, Katie crashes at my place.

The night before our flight to Vegas, Bob and Lisa throw a party, and since Chase has come to our place and isn't making a move to leave anytime soon, I invite him to come along with me and Katie to my brother's. Bob and Lisa have invited a ton of people, and I know they won't mind if I bring a sort of date. We walk into the party, Katie makes a beeline for the beer cooler, and I locate my brother. As I introduce him to Chase, I see Bob stiffen. He mumbles a greeting, frowns at Chase's fishy handshake, and then Chase heads off to get us beers. As soon as Chase is out of sight, Bob whispers, "What the fuck, Theresa? Who is this guy? He's older than I am."

"I don't think so—"

"He is. He's old as shit and out of shape. What the hell are you thinking?"

"Don't worry. I got this."

"Just looking out for my sister."

Drunker than I've ever seen her, Katie spends the night throwing up in my bathroom and passing out curled up on the living-room couch. Not having had a sip of alcohol, I too spend the night throwing up. When morning comes, I shake Katie, who's out cold, her arms strangling a throw pillow. She wakes up, stares at me, sits up, and sprints into the bathroom.

"Should be a fun plane ride," I say, following her.

I help her into her clothes, grab her go bag, and practically carry her outside.

"Seriously, can you do this?" I ask her. "It's a small plane."

"I love small planes," she says, whipping around and throwing up into the bushes.

The flight to Vegas starts bumpy and gets worse, and I vomit continually into a paper sack, Katie passed out in her seat, while Monica the good-natured volleyball player rubs my back. My anxiety peaks when we arrive at our hotel, and I take in the sleeping arrangements in our vast and garish room overlooking the Strip: two king-sized beds, one for Katie and Monica, the other for Chase and me. I'm not ready for this. He's nice and generous, but I'm not *that* into him. Not yet. Maybe not ever.

I get along well with Monica, and I have a blast with Katie, but I remain stressed all weekend and throw up more than usual. When we crash for the night, I inch as far away from Chase as possible on the bed. He doesn't seem to mind, or at least he doesn't say anything. His mood darkens only once all weekend, meaning he goes quiet, when I come out of the bathroom after throwing up for the fourth time that day.

After the weekend, back at my house, my roommates out for the evening, Chase and I order Chinese takeout and sit at the kitchen table. We don't say anything for a while, but I can feel Chase's eyes on me as I pick through some gooey vegetable dish with a single chopstick.

"So, are you okay?" he asks.

"Yeah, why?"

"Well, it's just that I've been noticing you seem to have a problem, a little bit, with eating."

I don't look at him. I keep poking through the vegetables as if I'm searching for gold.

"I had a girlfriend in college who had an eating thing," he says. "Another volleyball player."

I raise my head and meet his eyes, and before I can catch myself, I blurt, "Yes, I do struggle with eating. I throw up sometimes."

"Same as her. She had this thing called bulimia."

Bulimia.

The word strikes me like a slap.

Bulimia.

I wonder . . . *is that what I have?* It sounds so official.

"I don't think that's what I have," I say. "No, I don't have that."

I push the carton of Chinese food away, lay down my chopstick, and wrap my arms across my chest. "I struggle sometimes, that's all."

"She got through it," Chase says. He suddenly reaches across the table and tenderly caresses my arm. "You're a strong woman. You can get through it too."

The next evening, I come out of the bathroom after throwing up and find Dr. Martin—Lorraine—sitting on my bed.

"Theresa," she says gently, "are you throwing up?"

I don't answer at first, then I go into default denial mode. "No, why would you think that?"

"Well, I'm not tracking you or anything, but you spend an awful lot of time in the bathroom. And you've been eating my food. My ice cream. I go for a late-night snack and the entire pint is missing."

"I'm sorry. I wasn't even conscious I was doing that. I'll replace it."

"You know that's not the point."

I sit next to her on the bed. "Yes," I say. "I'm struggling with eating."

"Do you throw up a lot?"

"Quite a bit. I—"

I cry softly, wiping my nose with a tissue Lorraine hands me. "I can't figure out how to stop," I say.

"I know it's hard," she says. "I had friends in college who struggled with eating." She pauses. "You need help."

"I can't tell anybody about this," I say.

"I have a friend, a psychiatrist. I think you should talk to her. You need to take care of this now."

The tears come in streams now, and I grip Lorraine's arm. "I have to deploy," I say. "I've worked too hard with my Marines. I've come too far. I put my whole life into this."

"Okay, look, we're going to keep it off the books for now. Let's see how it goes. But check in with me."

"I will. Thank you."

I can handle this, I think. *I will take care of this.*

I'm a warrior.

>>>

I see Lorraine's friend. She has little experience with eating disorders but, after our first couple of sessions, determines that I need to deal with my stress issues and prescribes anti-anxiety medication. After a week of taking these pills, I feel less on edge, and I don't throw up as much. One night, I sit down again with Lorraine to give her an update. "I'm making progress," I tell her.

"I'm relieved. But Theresa—" She hesitates. "Look, I have to brief the battalion CO. I have to. You understand?"

"What are you going to say?"

"I have to report your . . . situation."

I say nothing.

"As long as you continue seeking help, it'll be okay," she says.

I don't know exactly what Lorraine says to the battalion CO, but I know she tells him that I am struggling with eating issues, that I'm dealing with it professionally, working to get the situation under control. I also know that she doesn't say the words *"eating disorder."*

"I want you to step it up," she says. "I want you to go to a support group, off base. I have a couple of choices for you."

"Sure, okay, I'll do that," I say.

"Theresa," Lorraine says, her voice rising, "I put myself on the line for you. You have to do this."

"I will."

"I'm serious," she says.

"I am too."

And I am, but as the time to deploy gets closer, my mind flies into a kind of frenzy. I can't shut it down. I walk around feeling a jolt of electricity with every step. I think about deployment constantly. My Marine mind-set takes over. Going to war. That's all that occupies my thoughts. I am a Marine. Marines do war. That's what we do. That's who I am.

I justify my eating struggle. I refuse to label it an eating disorder. I reject the term *bulimia*. I throw up. So what? That's how I deal. This behavior is not uncommon. Athletes, entertainers, high achievers throw up all the time. Football players puke in the locker room before a big game. Actors barf backstage before their Broadway debut. Singers throw up before performing at the Met or Carnegie Hall. You hear this story over and over. You *deal*. I'm not peeing blood or vomiting bile. I'm having trouble eating a muffin. It's ridiculous. I can handle this. I am handling this.

I will deploy.

»»»

I run a two-day, two-night field operation exercise, the XO briefing me in the field, allowing me two hours to prepare. I lead more than a hundred Marines, only three of them women. I create a five-paragraph order with Adam and Rigsbey, and with them standing over me and the squad leaders gathering around, I kneel on the ground. Using a stick and some rocks, I outline a battlefield and scratch our positions into the dirt.

"Here's what we're gonna do," I say. "We're gonna place land mines here and jersey barriers here, then we'll set up the obstacle plan like so. We have to set up the forward operating base here, so we'll need barbed wire, concrete barriers, and bunkers all along that perimeter. Now the snipers. I have you set up here, the minimum standoff distance from the land mines—"

I look up, take in the Marines around me.

"Are you guys getting this?"

A chorus of "yes, ma'am."

I go over the five-paragraph order, keeping my instructions to less than ten minutes, which I've learned from experience is the maximum amount of time most Marines can pay attention without fidgeting or drifting off into space.

I stand and finish delivering my paragraph order. I wait for the XO, rocking on his heels in the back, to crap all over everything I've just said. He takes a step forward and cups his chin with his hand. "Very tight distance between the snipers and those land mines."

"Yes, sir, I know it seems so. But according to the rule and regulations handbook on how to build a land mine field, that is the minimum standoff distance. I can move the mines another ten yards, but based on the territory we're covering, I don't want us to be too spread out."

"I'll say this, to go that close, you gotta have some big brass . . ." He stops himself, looks at me as if he has just now noticed I'm a woman and, his voice cracking, says, "Ovaries."

Half of the hundred Marines laugh, the others cough, then the laughter and coughing dissolve into one long uncomfortable buzz.

"Yeah, anyway," he says. "No, I see where you're going with this."

He keeps his head down, his eyes pinned on the battlefield I've etched at his feet, and I realize—stunningly—that for the first time ever, the XO has given me a compliment.

"Thank you, sir," I say.

He says something else, but the words come out garbled, jammed in his throat like a fur ball.

I don't care. He told everybody in these two platoons that I have "some big brass ovaries." Can't get any better than that.

>>>

Three weeks before we deploy, my dad comes to stay with me for a week. I pick him up at the airport, and I'm shocked by his appearance. He seems to have aged ten years. He's lost weight, and he slumps when he walks. His face looks gaunt, and his skin has gone ghostly white.

"Are you okay?" I say when he gets into the car. "You look so pale."

"Stress of the job," he says.

"Do you exercise?" I say.

"Some. Not as much as I should."

"Are you eating?"

He glances at me without speaking, and I wonder if he looks so wasted because he's actually stressed over *me*. He doesn't answer. I change the subject, ask him about his flight.

We get into it over dinner.

"How are you doing?" he asks.

"Dealing with it. Getting some help. I honestly don't know if I'm anxious about deploying or—"

I let the words trail off.

"Or . . . ?"

My voice lowers. "Or if I have a problem."

He reaches across the table and grabs both my hands. He speaks with an urgency I've never heard before. "Theresa, why can't you just *stop*?"

"I want to," I say. I withdraw my hands and look away. "I can't."

We spend the next week packing my bags for Iraq and making trips back and forth to the storage locker I've rented. We work slowly, neither of us in any hurry, lingering sometimes in the garage where I box up my books, CDs, and softball trophies. My dad, usually taking the lead, mostly stands off to the side. I can't imagine what he's thinking as he watches me pack, but he seems frozen, unsure of what to do, what to say.

Behind me, I hear a muffled noise. I turn and see that my dad has dropped his head onto his chest and that he is crying. I start to go to him, but he waves me away. "I'm sorry," he says. "I didn't mean to—"

"It's okay."

"Theresa, please," he says furiously, his eyes dripping with tears. "Take care of yourself."

"I will, Dad."

"Please . . . *please* take care of yourself."

"I will. I promise."

"I'm going to pray for you every day." He spreads his arms into what looks like a gesture of helplessness. I go to him and hug him, holding him, rocking him, listening to him sob, my heels resting against a carton full of books and trophies, mementos from high school and college, mementos from some other life, from some other *person*, and I think, *I will . . . I will come back alive and well.*

>>>

A few days before I deploy, Chase comes over to say goodbye and wish me well. We talk casually, not really mentioning my deployment. I don't feel a sense of urgency or finality, since Chase will be in Ramadi while I'm in Fallujah, and I may have an opportunity to see him in Iraq. I have a strong sense that he wants to stay the night, but I don't want him here. I need to finish my last-minute packing, and I want to make several phone calls. I'm on edge, but instead of trying to find ways to relax and slow down, I want to keep in motion. I don't want quiet or calm. I want activity. I want the time to pass. And I want to be alone. Chase and I hug, and he clings to me, and while he does, I think, with some confusion and embarrassment, *I'm glad he's leaving.*

The night before I deploy, my brothers call. I'm relieved to say our goodbyes over the phone and not in person. On the phone we can all pretend to be cool and tough hard-core Marines, one heading to Iraq, the others offering your typical hoorah pep talk— *watch your ass and you'll do fine* peppered with *the seven months will fly by* bullshit. I know how they really feel. Bob has already let it slip that combat engineers live in the heart of the shit, that they are sent everywhere, at any time, and are the ones most likely to come home in a body bag. Paul tries to pump me up by saying a lot of positive stuff, more well-meant clichés, not one word of which penetrates my skull. For my part, I'm happy that I'm able to suck it up and not cry, the main reason I'm glad we're saying goodbye on the phone. They tell me they love me. They say they're proud of me. And I know that they're scared shitless for me.

In the morning I wake up with a nasty cold. I top off my carry-on bag with a few last-second items, a book, a journal, toiletries, cold medicine, and then I do one last sweep of the house, making sure I haven't forgotten anything. I go back into my bedroom, and before I grab my bags, I go into the bathroom. I lock the door, lower the toilet seat lid, sit down, and scan this small room, which has been night after night—sometimes as often as three or four times a night—my safe place, my haven, my sanctuary. I would retreat in here, and I would hide and live my secret. I would run the water, turn on the fan, and purge my sins. I would purge my pain. I would purge my *life*. After I turned off the water and the fan and left the bathroom, I inevitably felt guilty and anxious. Most of all, I no longer felt safe.

Finally ready to leave, I enter the kitchen and find my roommates waiting. The woman I never really got to know wishes me good luck and hugs me. Lorraine walks me outside.

"So this is it," she says, the screen door singing and slamming behind us.

"Yep. Seven months, they say."

She nods. "You ready?"

"I was born ready," I say, grinning.

"You know what I mean."

"I know." I exhale. "I am ready. Been working hard."

"Have you had many . . . incidents?"

"A few," I say. "Not lately, though."

"Good," she says.

Of course, I mean *lately* as a relative term.

I have had my moments. I've gone days without throwing up, and I've had days when I've thrown up three times. I have discovered that the key is to compartmentalize. As long as I focus on being in the moment, on dealing with what is right in front of me, keeping my eating struggle separate from everything else, I will succeed.

"Well," I say to Lorraine as I prepare to stow my stuff in the awaiting van that will take me to the base. "Thank you."

"Take care of yourself, Theresa," she says. "I'll be thinking about you."

We hug briefly, and to my shock, I sniffle and have to knock back the tears. I pull away and reach for a packet of tissues in the pocket of my cammies. "I have a cold," I say.

Lorraine nods, and I see then that her eyes have filled up too.

⫸

At the base, I walk among more than one hundred Marines in the combined platoons, watching wives, mothers, sisters, girlfriends, and other family members and friends hugging and crying, a few losing it completely, wailing, clinging to the young Marines. A few of the Marines break down, but most hold it together, then with the well-wishers waving and shouting, we shuttle to the airstrip in a caravan of buses and fly to Germany, where we'll lay over a night. Then on to Kuwait for several days so we can adjust to the climate and time zone of the Middle East and be briefed on the rules of engagement and local customs. AC-130 will then fly us to Camp Fallujah for seven months of desert warfare, our mission to build obstacles, provide protection, and support our infantry.

I find my seat on the plane, lean my M16 rifle and my pistol into my body, and immediately start coughing. I reach under my seat, grab my carry-on, fish out a bottle of cough medicine, and chug it. Within minutes, the medicine knocks me out cold. Ten hours later, I wake up in Germany.

The next day, unable to breathe, my head socked with congestion, my heart pounding from nerves, a newly minted warrior, I step onto the tarmac in Kuwait.

14

DREAMLAND

JULY–DECEMBER 2005 / FALLUJAH

WE SPEND A WEEK CLUMPED TOGETHER AT A military base in Kuwait, the country a landscape of blazing heat and stony nighttime silence. As my head cold clears up, I attend classes every morning and afternoon.

We learn a few essential words in Arabic—"hello," "goodbye," "stop," "go back," "gun," and "bomb"—and we learn hand signals to use when we don't have the words. We go over the rules of engagement, starting with never firing on the enemy unless the enemy fires on us first. We learn what to expect when we get in-country, what behavior we will see. We learn about Iraqi culture. I hear for the first time that Iraqi men treat their women like property. Our instructor tells us that when we see a group of Iraqis walking, the men will always be behind the women. That way, if they come upon a land mine, the women will step on the mine first.

I'm so stunned by this, I ask the instructor to repeat it. When he does, I confess to the room that I'm having a little trouble processing this information.

"Oh, you'll see a lot of things that will be difficult to process," the instructor says. "I can promise you that."

Each day the hours click by slowly, interminably, and we wait. When I'm not working out or in class, I keep to myself. I mainly hole up in my room and read. I zip through *It's Not About the Bike* and find myself identifying with Lance Armstrong and his battle with cancer. Everyone struggles, I realize. I tell myself that if he can get through freaking testicular cancer, I can get through my little eating issue. Lance becomes my role model. I finish the book brimming with new resolve. I vow to stop throwing up. I decide that since I'm literally in a new world, I will enter a new world figuratively. The entire time we spend in Kuwait, I don't throw up at all.

Then we leave. We fly to Fallujah in the middle of the night. With Rigsbey, I help herd my Marines into our rumbling C-130, then we take off and fly low for an hour, the plane rattling and shaking so violently that almost everyone on it throws up, including me.

We land, gather our gear, pour out of the C-130, and pile into a line of idling Humvees that bring us to our barracks. As we drive, I notice the light, a fuzzy pale gold that hangs like a curtain, even in the night. Voices follow us, too, an off-key chanting that in the dark unnerves me. Everything seems so . . . foreign. I know how ridiculous that sounds, but on this drive, sitting in the front seat of the Humvee, it hits me that this is *real*. This is not a field exercise. We are not simulating Iraq in the scrubby, dusty hills above Camp Pendleton. We are here. Those voices are not pumped in over speakers from someone's iPod. Those voices come from Iraqis in prayer. The clump of buildings in the distance makes up downtown Fallujah, the buildings mostly low and flat except for a few taller, rounder buildings, some with colorful towers, scattered throughout. Mosques, I realize, are where the chanting comes from. *Prayers*, I think, *at three o'clock in the morning?* The voices swell. I close my eyes and try to shut them out. I can't.

The Humvees enter Camp Fallujah through a side gate, then stop, and we climb down. Disoriented, I take a moment to breathe and follow my gunny toward the barracks. I locate my room, which is surprisingly spacious, large enough for a twin bed, dresser, bookcase, and desk, right across the hall from my gunny and platoon guide and down the hall from the platoon commander and captain. I instinctively inspect my bathroom, which is inconveniently located outside, and find it clean considering we're on a military base in the Iraqi desert, but lacking a secure lock. Anticipating . . . worrying . . . that I will soon need a private place, a safe place, I scour the area for better bathroom accommodations and find only a row of Porta-Potties. I return to my room, stow my stuff, and then check every room, each with four Marines bunking together, making sure everyone has been accounted for and has settled in. Then, too jacked to sleep, I climb into bed and thumb through Mr. Armstrong's memoir, dutifully dog-earing pages and underlining passages.

〉〉〉

We call it Dreamland.

In the center of Camp Baharia, a smaller military base, sat a lake, placid and dreamlike. At Camp Baharia, back in the day, our military forces would supply the Iraqi army with water, Iraqi soldiers nuzzling huge tankers to the edge of the lake and filling them up. A year or so ago, insurgents overran the city. Our forces hit back hard with Operation Phantom Fury, shelling buildings, setting up snipers, clearing houses, killing 1,350 insurgents, and wounding hundreds more. Since it was larger, more centrally located, more protected, and ultimately more secure, Camp Fallujah became our go-to base. Camp Baharia fell into second position, its lake, for now, off-limits.

But the name—Dreamland—stuck.

And so I walk through this piece of Dreamland with Rigsbey, on the way to a meeting, today's temperature a balmy 107 degrees. I feel the heat writhe around me, sticking like a second skin. I walk slowly, deliberately, the air so thick I have to push through it. Every time I go outside, I feel assaulted by this heat, and I squint into what seems like a sandstorm, the air filmy and light brown. At first I considered the air to be a variation of LA smog, but this air is darker, more present, more ominous.

We pass a few Marines huddled in a courtyard smoking. They hardly look up as we go by. Earlier I saw several Marines taking turns playing video poker at a computer. I worry that my Marines have already become bored and complacent. I know that we have all begun a period of adjustment. We must acclimate to the heat, the sandy air, and a life lived on a ticking clock. We may go through hours, even days, of crushing monotony scorched by the paralyzing sun, but we must always be on alert for the alarm to sound. And it will sound.

Now, though, Rigsbey and I lope through the base toward our first assignment, sweat pooling up on my neck, my lips dry and starting to split. Without breaking stride, I swill some water from the canteen I carry wrapped in canvas and splash a few drops on my arms.

"Okay, it's a little warm," Rigsbey says.

"Yeah, but it's a dry heat," I say.

"I hear we can hit one-fifteen easy."

"Great. Maybe catch some rays, huh?"

"You make this shit almost tolerable. You have the best attitude."

"Fuck off," I say, laughing. We arrive at the Office of Human Intelligence and head to a desk at the far wall manned by a major in his late thirties, the officer in charge of the human intelligence platoon. Clunky, loud desk fans whir around us, blowing hot air, offering zero relief. The major sees us and stands. I blink and probably blush. The major looks exactly like George Clooney.

It must be the heat or the lack of food and the fact that I have resumed throwing up, but I suddenly feel like I'm going to faint. I grip the edge of his desk and hold on, the room rotating slowly.

"Are you okay, Lieutenant?" the major asks.

"Yes, sir. I'm so embarrassed. I'm not used to this heat—"

"Here," he says and slides a chair over.

I practically fall into it, mutter "thank you," and sip from a glass of water that materializes in front of me.

"Are you up for this today?" George Clooney asks.

"Yes, sir, I'm all right." I catch my breath. Mercifully, the room steadies. I look up. "So, okay, sir, what do you need for your office?"

As engineers, we build, and our assignment—my first assignment in Fallujah—is to build this guy a new office, a freestanding structure, his own personal SWA hut. My captain has warned me that the major can be picky. Or, as he put it, a pain in the ass.

"Here's what I'm thinking." The major sits back down at this desk and pyramids his fingers. Rigsbey opens a notebook and hands me a yellow legal pad and pen. We both lean forward, pens poised.

"I'm thinking skylight," the major says.

I glance at Rigsbey and see him scribbling furiously. I turn back to the major, the light-headedness returning. I power through it. Another breath and I knock the fuzz out of my head. "You want a skylight in your SWA hut?"

"I want light. Lots of light. And the light here . . ."

It looks like sand, I think.

"Mesmerizing," the major says, looking off to nowhere. "Intoxicating."

"Skylight," I say, pretending to write it down. "What else?"

"I envision a sort of suite. Couple, three rooms, a front room, maybe a loft . . ."

"A *loft*?"

"Is that an issue?"

"It might be a shade fancy for an SWA hut. Not sure if we're capable of—"

"You're engineers, right? I don't see a loft as a problem."

"What about a sunken living room?"

"I like that."

"I was kidding, sir."

"Wish list, right? Why not?"

"Sure."

"I made a list of a few things that I will need, though, accoutrements." He slides a sheet of paper across the desk toward me.

"A toaster oven," I read. "Microwave, dishwasher, humidifier, dehumidifier." I look up. "Never could figure out the difference." I look back at his list and continue reading. "Espresso machine, La-Z-Boy recliner . . . *hot tub*?"

"*Wish* list," he repeats.

I look at Rigsbey, who has bowed his head to keep from laughing.

"Is that it?" I ask the major.

"I think so."

"Well, okay." I stand abruptly. "I'll just run your requests by my captain, make sure we have this stuff in stock and that we have the proper building supplies."

"He'll be fine with everything, right?"

"Oh, he's very accommodating."

>>>

"Tell this guy to go pack sand."

An hour later, Rigsbey and I sit across from the captain in his hot, cluttered office. The captain—my height, hyper, in constant motion, his hair gone prematurely white—springs to his feet. He paces, shakes his head. "Who does he think he is? A skylight? A loft? We're not doing any of that shit. You know what we're gonna do? The bare minimum."

"What do I tell him?"

"I told you. Tell him to go pack sand."

"I'm a lower rank. I can't tell him to do that, sir. Now, if *you* wanted to tell him to go pack sand—"

"Get out of here. We've got a whole list of jobs to do."

I tell the major that because of time restraints and a minimum of supplies, we're building him a standard SWA hut, nothing special, no skylight, no loft, no hot tub, no humidifiers, no espresso machine, nothing on his wish list. As I break the news to him, he offers up a shy, aw-shucks grin. "I kind of thought that's all you could do," he says, noticing that I've written down exactly none of his requests.

>>>

For the first week or two, we attend meetings each day at 0900.

I wake at 0600, work out in the grimy gym next to the barracks, shower, and go to breakfast, usually sitting with the captain and the lieutenant from operations. I control my food here, managing eggs, cereal, or pancakes, chasing down my meal with a mug of tepid coffee. After breakfast, the three of us walk the short distance to the COC, Center of Communications, and gather for a briefing with other officers from District Battalion Eighth, fifteen or twenty of us crammed into a stuffy room with dim lighting that sometimes flickers and no fans. We discuss forthcoming missions, logistics, safety, local politics, rumors of mortar attacks, the exodus of insurgents from Fallujah to Ramadi, concern about the insurgents who stayed behind, the upcoming elections in December. Despite the lack of air circulating in the hot room, nobody dozes. The tension in the room is too high. I'm fidgety, on edge, my leg pumping. I take notes, I ask questions, I await orders, I search faces. I am the only woman.

After these meetings, I walk through the base and become acquainted with as many Marines as I can. My routine varies. I stay behind at COC, or head over to human intelligence, or wander over to administration, or monitor job sites. I make it a point to stop by the construction of the major's SWA hut and check if everything's proceeding on schedule.

I introduce myself to everyone I encounter. I shoot the shit, try to keep people engaged. I often jump in and help with the work—transporting wood, hammering nails, hauling gear. I hear from more than one person that they look forward to my visits.

"You're so happy," an admin officer says to me. "You're such a shining light here."

I'm flattered, but I feel that I'm just doing my job.

During our free time in the afternoons, I answer e-mails, stop by the PX or the post office, or go to the phone center to call my dad, Chase, or my brothers. I hold visiting hours, keeping my door open. Marines confide in me, confess to me. I hear about marital problems, fears, homesickness. One Marine tells me she's considering becoming a nun. After I close my door, I generally skip dinner or eat something light and turn in early. I flip open my computer, tool around the Internet, and discover the show *24*, devouring every episode.

And every night, like clockwork, feeling achingly lonely and empty, I throw up into my trash can.

$$\text{⦚⦚⦚}$$

Game on.

I run convoys. We deliver food or supplies. We build obstacles, checkpoints, watchtowers, SWA huts. We camp out two or three nights in the desert, in the war zone.

The convoys vary from two ten-ton trucks to fifteen trucks, plus the communication vehicle where I ride, a tricked-out Humvee with GPS, its snazzy monitor showing my position as a blinking blue dot, a two-way radio, a satellite phone, a set of walkie-talkies.

Before each convoy, I receive coordinates and navigation, which include hot spots to avoid. I talk over the plan with Rigsbey, work up a five-paragraph order, and go over all the details with my captain. Then the captain and I confer with the intelligence officer, come up with a final plan and a backup plan. I pass this on to my communications officer, who puts both the primary route and the secondary route into the GPS. Then, depending on the nature of the mission, my gunny and I decide how many Marines we'll need and choose which ones. In some ways I feel like a film director, only instead of casting a movie, I'm casting a mission.

Rigsbey and I select Marines based on their effectiveness, enthusiasm, and work ethic, as well as whether they have a problem with a woman leading them. Some men do. They never say anything directly to me, but I can tell. I want to eliminate these Marines from the convoy for that reason alone. But my commitment to the mission trumps that feeling. I will go with talent over anything. I need the most accomplished builders, the best engineers, the top .50 cal machine gunners or AT4 shooters in the unit perched atop the Humvee. I press my rank and my authority. I give off a vibe. The vibe says clearly, "I don't care if you have an issue with me because I'm a woman. You're going to listen to me. This is how we do."

It works. Word spreads. Marines know that one false step, one snide eye roll, one ounce of hostility I pick up, and I will bust you down so fast you'll spend the rest of your deployment pushing papers behind a desk in some sweaty, smelly hut, fuck your talent.

I'm upbeat on base, everybody's friend, Ms. Congeniality, but once we're on a mission, I go all business. I take personal responsibility for every Marine I lead. I live by this phrase, every word, every syllable: *Trust me, follow me, or die.*

》》》

An hour before dawn, I take out my first convoy, seven trucks and my Humvee riding lead as we stop at the gate to check out. The Marine at the checkpoint looks over the work roster I hand him and then stares at me, the look on his face a mix of confusion and surprise.

"What's the matter?" I ask. "Something wrong?"

"No, no, no." He peers at the paperwork, gazes up at me, and frowns.

"You look like you're in shock," I say. "You need a salt tablet?"

"Oh, no, I just, you know, never saw a woman leave the wire before. Especially a woman in charge."

"Well, here you go. I'll be your first."

"Ha, okay, yeah."

"Everything check out?"

"Yes, ma'am."

"See you in two days."

We're gone.

I allow two trucks to pass, the Humvee slides into the third position, and the convoy heads out, avoiding downtown Fallujah, a potential hive for snipers and insurgents on the lam who have been known to flee their cells and throw themselves at convoys, bombs strapped to their chests. I've been given a straightforward mission my first time out: a delivery, a night drop of supplies, food, and building materials, two days, two nights, a quick turnaround.

My stomach, empty from throwing up and queasy with excitement, rumbles with every bump, pothole, and pebble we hit on the road. We navigate away from dirt roads, which kick up dust and sand, making it difficult to see the road ahead and possible land mines. This day, for some reason, the paved road we travel is jammed with cars. It feels like an LA freeway at rush hour. We lower our speed to a crawl, falling seriously behind schedule.

I drive with a communications Marine, a reservist, whom I get to know well. His given name is Bradley, but we call him Tampon because before he deployed, when he was a reserve, he served once a month.

Tampon runs the two-way radio, keeps us connected to base and the other trucks in the convoy, and handles all the technology in the Humvee. He indicates that an officer from the COC wants me and hands me a headset. I slip it on and hear, "Wildcat, 1-4, come in."

"Roger, this is Wildcat, over."

"Why aren't you there yet?"

"There's so much fucking traffic. Plus we had to slow down because someone's fucking vegetable wagon broke down, and they had to push the fucking thing to the side of the road."

"You're coming in broken and unreadable. Repeating. Why aren't you at the location yet?"

I speak slower and louder. *"Because . . . there . . . is . . . fucking . . . traffic."*

A crackling high-pitched blast of static burns my eardrums. I rip off my headset and turn to Tampon. "My fucking ears are bleeding. What's wrong with this thing?"

"Must be the connection. I'll fix it. But, ma'am, you really shouldn't swear on the radio. It's kind of a rule."

"You're right. I fucking forgot."

He roars.

We arrive at our destination an hour late. We unload the convoy and set up camp for the night. Tomorrow we will help build a watchtower and, once nightfall hits, return to base. Tonight I walk among the Marines, checking in, seeing if anyone needs anything. I radio back to base, manage to report our progress without cursing. I head back to camp to catch a few hours of sleep. Before I do, I take a detour. I walk to a secluded spot and throw up. Walking back to camp, my body quivering, I scream at my demon. *Leave me alone.* I don't want to throw up. I have to. I run two or three convoys a week.

I keep to paved roads whenever possible. The first time I take a dirt road, a lump of fear rises in my throat. The captain, my staff sergeant, and my platoon guide warn me to avoid dirt roads for two compelling reasons: one, it's easier for insurgents to lay land mines; two, you cannot *see.* Now my convoy, ten trucks snaking, the first of two back-to-back ten-truck convoys sent from base, lumbers through the dirt, small dust storms swirling, cones of pebbles and sand slamming into our windshields. Binoculars pressed to my eyes, I case the vicinity for trouble. I see only a barren, desolate desert, heat rising from the surface like clouds of steam. The landscape looks empty, dead, ominous. Later, back at base, I hear that a suicide bomber ran at our sister convoy, the other ten-trucker, no more than fifteen minutes behind us. The suicide bomber blew himself up before he reached the trucks.

"Talked to people who saw it," Tampon tells me. "Guts flying everywhere."

"Fortunately he didn't plan well," I say.

"For real."

That night, alone in my room, I picture the suicide bomber charging the convoy. If he had waited thirty seconds, he might have blown up at least one truck, possibly two, maybe more.

My head stabbing, my stomach growling, I can't help thinking, *That could've been us.*

That could have been us.

>>>

My captain and I take a convoy on a day trip to Ferris Town to do some reconnaissance for a major building project involving a watchtower and a vehicle checkpoint. The road we take sucks, much of it dirt, divots, and crevices, putting me on edge until we finally get to Ferris Town. Once there, we scope out the town— empty, sad buildings and homes, a few scattered mosques, scrawny children and stray dogs cluttering the streets. We determine how many Marines we'll need for the job and meet with the Iraqi leadership to pull permits and make nice, the Iraqi politicians scowling at me the whole time. Women don't normally attend meetings of any sort in this country, and being tall and blond and buff, I'm sure I look like a freak. Mission accomplished, we drive back to base on the same dirt road, this time at night, each bump and jolt jostling my nerves.

The next day a second convoy leaves for Ferris Town to deliver equipment and supplies and begin building prep. On the same dirt road, this convoy spots a land mine poking out of a freshly dug hole in the ground. Using the proper protocol, the squad leader calls in EOD—the Explosive Ordinance Disposal Unit—to remove the land mine. The EOD team arrives and begins investigating the land mine, determining how to diffuse it. They don't realize that this land mine is a decoy. The truck loaded with explosives, where the convoy's corpsman rides, backs up over a second, hidden land mine, this one real and live. The ten-ton truck explodes into a fireball, jumps off the dirt ground, and somersaults, spewing metal in every direction, incinerating the corpsman.

I hear the story in an emergency briefing that night.

After the captain finishes relaying the details, the room goes stony silent and cold, despite the oppressive heat bearing down on us.

I don't know the corpsman well. I did have a short conversation with him on one of my spontaneous base walk-throughs. Didn't. *Didn't* know him well. Past tense. A wife and three kids. When I met him, he slid pictures out of his wallet.

In the briefing room, the captain speaks in a hush, his words carefully chosen, something about a memorial service, something about the casualties of war, something about losing a good man.

My mouth goes dry. I choke back a sob. This war. These wars. I'm fighting two wars. I know that now. One war outside, in hell. The other war in my own private hell. My war within.

>>>

One morning, the regimental commander, Colonel Quinn, taller than me, black hair, dark eyes, waits for me at breakfast. He invites me to join him and chooses a table by the far wall. He steers the conversation toward my background—college, softball, family— the whole time peering at me with unblinking eyes.

That afternoon the captain calls me into his office. Colonel Quinn has ordered me to report to him at 2300 hours.

"You're needed," the captain says. "Bring your weapon and your gear."

"What am I doing?"

"Can't say."

"Will I be staying overnight?"

"No. It's a night mission. Could go all night, though, I'm told. I still expect you to report tomorrow morning for work as usual."

"Yes, sir."

"Sleep is highly overrated," the captain says.

I arrive at the regimental commander's office at 2300 hours as instructed, gripping my go bag, cradling my M16 and my pistol. The office is empty. I sit on the edge of a chair and wait.

After about an hour, the colonel enters through the outside door. I stand at attention. He looks me over for a second and says, "Do you know martial arts?"

"Yes, sir."

"All right, good." He thrusts his chin forward and speaks rapidly. "Delta Force has disrupted a cell. They captured seven insurgents—six men, one woman."

I raise an eyebrow.

"The men are ours to keep. But we have to return the woman to the CMOC, hand her over to the mayor of Fallujah. We're doing an *exchange*."

He makes a face, as if the word has curdled in his mouth.

"An exchange, sir?"

"Yes. We bring this woman insurgent to the mayor, and in exchange, he won't shut down the elections."

He thrusts his chin in my direction this time. "You will be the insurgent's escort. Except for her husband, a man is not allowed to touch an Iraqi woman. She's not married."

"A woman is a man's property, sir," I say.

"You got it," he says.

"So we're returning some guy's property."

"You're a quick study," the colonel says. "You're in charge of the prisoner."

The colonel and I drive to the Fallujah airfield. He parks next to a Humvee where two Marines wait. He says something to the first Marine, who nods and goes into a darkened building. Less than a minute later, the marine comes out of the building, leading a very short woman, not even five feet tall, who's dressed in a burka from head to toe, her face almost completely covered in cloth and shadow. The Marine steers her by her elbow. She steps warily, unsteadily, and as she approaches, I see that a blindfold covers her eyes and her wrists are handcuffed in front of her. The Marine walks to the Humvee and, as gently as he can, maneuvers her into the backseat. The Marine closes the door and joins the colonel and me outside his Humvee.

"All right, Lieutenant, you're the only one who touches her the rest of the way," Colonel Quinn says to me.

"Yes, sir."

The colonel gives a go signal and climbs into the back of the first Humvee. I get into the passenger seat of the second Humvee, three of us in here now—the driver, the insurgent, and me. The colonel's vehicle heads down the alley, and we follow, going off base, toward the wail of discordant prayer chanting and the crack of mortar fire.

We keep off the main highway, driving on back roads to the CMOC—the Civil Military Operations Center—a complex at the outskirts of Fallujah City. At first, nobody speaks, the only sound the grumble of the engine and the grind of tires on the road. After about ten minutes, I can't take it. I need to fill the silence. I'm wired, nervous, and a little weak and dizzy from throwing up twice this evening before I left my barracks. I ask the driver about himself. Where he's from. How long he's been in. Family. Interests. I tell him a bit about me. After about thirty minutes, the absurdity of this hits us both. We're two combat Marines in Iraq transporting a female terrorist in the middle of the night, and we're bullshitting like a couple of buddies from The Basic School.

Feels right, actually. Feels necessary. Feels . . . human.

I still do my job. I check the insurgent in the backseat every thirty seconds, gauging her every movement. She doesn't move at all. She's a statue. At one point, I lean over the seat to confirm her breathing. Her breaths come in small, muted puffs. Occasionally I hear a soft sound, almost like a purr. I can't see her lips beneath the folds of her burka, but I wonder if she is praying.

After an hour, the driver pulls the Humvee off the road and parks next to a large barn of a building that looks like it could be a civic center in an American town. I scramble out of the vehicle, fling open the back door, and tap the insurgent lightly on the shoulder. She jumps, growls something in her language, and whips her head away from me, facing the opposite door.

"Let's go," I say, and grip her under her arm. She makes that purring sound again, hesitates, but doesn't resist. She allows me to lead her out of the Humvee. I cup her head with my hand so she won't bash the doorframe and walk her into the building.

We enter a cavernous, brightly lit auditorium filled with rows of worn chairs. As we walk, light from the grid of fluorescent bulbs overhead bounces off the white walls, causing me to squint.

I lead the insurgent by her arm toward a conference table at the front of the room, where the colonel, three Marine officers, and four Iraqis stand. As soon as the Iraqis see me and the insurgent, they stop talking and follow our progress down the center aisle. We walk slowly, the short woman shuffling, moving awkwardly. We arrive in front of the men at the table, and I can see that the Iraqis, none of whom is taller than six feet, are staring at me. I restrain the insurgent, my hand holding her in place by the arm, keeping her from slamming into the table. She weaves slightly, raising her head toward the ceiling and the blinding light.

One of the Iraqis, the man in charge, perhaps the mayor, says something to the man next to him—the translator, I assume—who in turn whispers something to the colonel.

"Take off her blindfold," the colonel says to me.

I reach for the blindfold, and as soon as my fingertips touch the cloth, the woman flinches. I hold for a beat, say, "It's okay," as if she can understand me, and then as carefully as I can, I slide the blindfold down and pull it away, seeing her face for the first time. She's young, about my age, and she's pretty. She looks around the room, her eyes blinking furiously, then looks up at me.

Her eyes go wide. She gapes at me, her mouth opening and closing like a fish. She has clearly never seen a woman my size.

The major again confers with the translator, who speaks to the colonel. He tells me to sit the prisoner down and to offer her a glass of water from a pitcher on the table. I bring her to a chair, her movements slower, clumsier, her eyes fastened on me. She sits at the table and places her handcuffed hands in front of her. I pour a glass of water from the pitcher and hold the glass to her lips.

She spits out the water.

The Iraqi mayor shouts something. The prisoner turns her head, water dribbling down her chin. The colonel wags his head at a chair facing her and I sit down, my weapon at my side. The prisoner and I sit opposite each other, for what turns out to be two hours.

The longest two hours of my life.

As I sit, the colonel and the mayor negotiate the terms of the insurgent's release. They speak civilly, without raising their voices, and as they work out the details of this woman's fate, I think about her. She keeps her eyes open, looking off, beyond me, her eyes small brown dots, sometimes wide and frightened, sometimes glazed over and weary. *Who is she?* I wonder. What is her life like? Does she have a family, a boyfriend, someone who loves her? What is she feeling right now? Is she afraid? Does she think of herself as a freedom fighter or a martyr? Or does she think she is a victim? Is she at all happy, or content? I wonder what will happen to her.

I wonder if we would get along. What would it have been like if we had met under different circumstances? Would we have been able to talk? Is there any shot that we could've been friends?

I think then that this is fucked. All of it. I know we're arguing about how to save the upcoming elections, but what about this woman's freedom? In this country, she's not even a person. She's property. No different than this table. I bat these thoughts away. I'm afraid I will shout them. Instead, I resign myself to this realization: maybe it's not all fucked, but this young woman is fucked. She's trapped. I know the feeling.

It's ironic. We're in different places, on different sides, yet neither of us has any choice. My world is supposedly all about choices, but I wonder if the only real choice I have is the choice I've made to throw up. Ultimately, here we are, the hotshot lieutenant and the doomed insurgent, and we will both do what these men tell us. That is the way of both our worlds. I imagine then that she will be executed. She will become a martyr.

When an Islamic male martyrs himself, he reputedly receives the pleasures of seventy-two virgins in the afterlife.

What does a female martyr get?

The negotiation completed, the elections saved, the colonel and the mayor shake hands, and the colonel tells me that we can go. I stand and give the young woman a last glance. She turns away, dragging her cuffed hands through the small pool of water that remains on the table.

"Well, we dodged a bullet," the colonel says outside. "What time do you have to report?"

"Leading a convoy at 0800."

He peers at his watch. "Looks like you might be able to catch an hour of sleep."

"More than enough, sir."

The colonel actually chuckles. "I'll be calling on you again."

That night I get zero sleep. I shower, dress, wolf down breakfast, a bunch of crap I don't want, keep eating, more food than I can handle—more food than most linemen can handle—hit the latrine, throw up, feel like *shit*, start to crash, amp myself up, get my ass to COC, plan my convoy, write my five-paragraph order, grab my platoon sergeant, cast my team, and run my convoy.

I'm a machine. I operate on adrenaline, on sense memory, on commitment. I feel I have no control of my life, no way to decompress, no place to let out my stress. I see no margin for error. I can make no mistakes. I must lead with supreme efficiency. I must be perfect.

Except I'm not perfect.

But . . . I can control what I eat, how much I eat, and how I get rid of it. As long as I do that, I'm okay, I'm good.

Marines drink. Some do drugs. I do food. My drug of choice.

The colonel calls on me three more times to escort insurgents from Camp Fallujah to CMOC, all after hours, each lasting all night before I run a convoy in the morning. I power through those days on sheer force of will. The midnight missions amp me up, boost my confidence. I feel like a genuine badass. I not only can do this, I can do it all. Bring. It. *On*. As long as I can take a few moments for myself—say, three, four, five times a day—to purge and to cleanse. Which I do. Without fail. Even though on this base, in this war, privacy is at a premium. In those moments, in my safe place, in the bathroom, after I throw up, I know I'm running on fumes. I know I'm working on false energy. And I know I'm living a lie.

I start writing frequently to my dad. I prefer letters to phone calls because I know that if I hear his voice, I'll break down. I write in stream of consciousness, purging myself emotionally on paper, expressing my fears, my increased eating struggles, my anxiety, my insane working hours, my exhaustion. I intend at first to remain newsy. I don't want him to worry. But I can't keep a lid on my feelings. My letters become increasingly desperate and urgent, unflinching cries for help. He writes back often, letters of concern. He suggests that I pray.

I go to chapel.

I sneak into the back of the small auditorium and take a seat on the aisle. I bow my head and try to lose myself in the service and the words of the chaplain. Afterward, when the few Marines who've attended the service have gone, I stay by myself and pray. I pray that everyone here will be safe. I pray that I will make the right decisions. I pray for a clear, calm mind.

I can't think of anything else to pray for.

I decide to talk to the chaplain. I don't make an appointment. I pop in one day when he's sitting at his desk and ask if I can have a moment of his time. He hesitates, then points to a chair and tells me to sit down. He's a slight man in his forties, rumpled even in uniform, and nervous. His bottom lip quivers when he talks. "What can I do for you?"

"I'm struggling with eating," I say, the words flying out of my mouth.

"Do you mean you have an eating disorder?"

"Yes," I say. "I think so." I pause and then I say, "I need some help."

"You're in a war."

I look at him until he turns away. "I'm not sure what you want me to do," he says.

I want you to give me strength. I want you to give me guidance. I want you to offer me solace.

I want you to pray with me.

"Nothing. I don't want you to do anything." I stand. "Thanks for your time."

My legs carry me out of his office, down the hall of his SWA hut, and outside into the glare of the sun. I feel momentarily lost. My stomach burns, as if I've been stabbed. I step into an open, sandy area, and I start walking without any idea where I'm going. I would stop if I could, but I can't. Nearly doubled over with pain now, I walk, wobbling, lurching, tears pouring down my face, my broken body reduced to taking one tiny step at a time . . . and then another . . . and another . . .

"Lieutenant? Lieutenant Hornick!"

Rigsbey.

I stop, mop the tears away with my sleeve. Somehow, sensation returns to my legs, the pain in my stomach ebbs, and I manage to turn around. My gunny stands fifty feet away, squinting into the sun, looking like a mirage. "We need to go."

"I know," I say, but I don't move.

"You okay?"

"Perfect," I say.

I begin walking back.

⟩⟩⟩

We build a vehicle checkpoint and a massive watchtower in Ferris Town, thirty-three Marines camping on site for ten days. I commute from Camp Fallujah to the building site, staying for three days at a time. I walk through the site like Mama Bear, pounding nails next to my Marines, poring over blueprints with them, hauling lumber together, making sure they're eating, getting enough sleep, taking appropriate breaks. At night, I sleep in the corner of an abandoned schoolhouse, bunking with my platoon sergeant, my platoon guide, and the one other female Marine on site. The first night I claim my cot, Rigsbey scratches his freshly shaved scalp, his eyes on his bed at the foot of mine.

"What's the matter?" I ask.

"Are you sure about these sleeping arrangements?"

"Why, what's wrong?"

"Well, you're a woman, last I checked, I'm a guy, last I checked—"

"Seriously? The captain's cool. He won't care."

"I'm more worried about the colonel."

"Don't worry about the colonel. I'll handle the colonel."

The colonel's not happy.

"You have to think of your image," he says on the way to escort my fourth insurgent. "What people might say."

"I do think about that, sir. But I refuse to take rooms away from my Marines. They're working so hard out there. I want them to be as comfortable as possible at night."

"It's your platoon," he says. "But my opinion? I don't think you should be bunking with the men."

When I get back to the barracks, the other female and I switch rooms with fifteen Marines who are occupying a large, comfortable space. They're clearly not happy. I can't help it. I know an order when I hear one.

The mayor of the local town threatens to shut down our power and cut off our water. Insurgents have been identified, and he wants us to prevent potential attacks and provide protection. In return, he promises to keep the utilities running. Of course, as I point out to Rigsbey, isn't this why we're building the watchtower and vehicle checkpoint, to provide protection? Shutting us down hurts the town and aids the insurgents.

"You know what makes sense in this country?" I ask Rigsbey as we ride in a Humvee in a three-truck convoy from the job site to CMOC in Ferris Town. "Nothing."

The mayor has insisted that he conduct the utilities negotiations with the officer in charge of the project. That would be me. But since I am a woman and Iraqis don't acknowledge women in positions of authority, I have pretended to switch rank with Rigsbey. He wears my lieutenant's bars and I wear his sergeant's stripes. I will sit back and stay silent in the meeting while my gunny negotiates the points we've discussed with the mayor.

I follow Rigsbey and a dozen other Marines into the barnlike auditorium at the CMOC. Twenty Iraqis await us at the table in the front of the room. As I walk in, every head swivels toward me. I read a mix of expressions on their faces, ranging from shock to disgust. I am, of course, the only woman in the room, and clearly the Iraqis don't want me here. I ignore the animosity I feel, avert my eyes from the roomful of stares, and take a seat. After a minute, a translator steps forward and introduces the two main players, Rigsbey and the mayor. The mayor is short, stumpy, and homely, his face creased and pockmarked. He leers at me, grinning with a mouthful of broken yellow teeth.

The negotiations go smoothly. The mayor seems satisfied with our promise of protection and orders his minister of utilities to maintain our power. Handshakes all around. I stand to leave and find myself looking down at the mayor, who blocks my way and tilts his head to look up at me.

"You are tall," he says in a thick accent. "Tall like a man."

I say nothing.

"I have four madams at home," he says, shooting me a lecherous yellow grin. His breath reeks. "*Four* madams."

"Back home I have five boyfriends. *Five*."

His mouth drops. "You cannot do that. You're a woman."

"I'm an American. I can do whatever the fuck I want."

>>>

I hang with the Marines at the construction site. I work out with them early every morning before the heat withers and wrecks us and then I help out wherever I can. At night we gather inside after dinner, playing cards, a board game, shooting the shit.

And I throw up. I make numerous visits to the bathroom, a nasty, oversize outhouse with three skinny stalls, each with a hole dug out for a toilet. Before I enter the bathroom, I hang the *"Women"* sign on the door and then I go in, carrying a plastic trash bag, but instead of doing my business in the bag, I throw up into it. Then I leave the latrine, switch the sign to *"Men,"* and toss the plastic bag into the fire pit. One night, after my third visit to the head, a Marine says, "Damn, you're going to the bathroom a lot. You okay, ma'am?"

"I'm not feeling well. I think it's something I ate."

"I hear *that*, ma'am."

>>>

One night, we talk about women.

Everybody knows that Iraqis think of women as pieces of property, but what sets me off is that some Marines think of women as pieces of meat. A few Marines admit that I have changed their thinking. I can hang with the guys, they say—hell, I'm fitter than half of them—and this has made them alter their mind-set when it comes to women in combat and women in general.

A few, though, view women purely as sex objects. Doesn't matter what a woman looks like, or whether they have any relationship with her at all, or what *she* wants; they would still have sex with her. Nothing matters at all except for the guy's sexual needs.

"That's one step away from rape," I say.

"We can't help it," a Marine says. "Guys are guys. We see a woman, we will want to do her. Especially if it's been a while."

"Like what, a couple of hours?"

A few snickers, but I can see that a lot of the Marines have a hard time dealing with women, especially with women out here in Dreamland, which means they have a hard time dealing with me.

Back at the base, a lieutenant from another platoon finds me in the admin office. He swallows before he speaks. "Listen, just so you know, and don't freak out, somebody wrote some bullshit about you on the bathroom wall."

"What was it?"

"Maybe you should look—"

"Just say it."

He lowers his voice and says, "I fucked Lt. Hornick."

I shake my head. "Thanks for telling me."

"Sorry," he says.

Well, I'm not all that surprised.

My brothers, especially Paul, warned me that Marines would start rumors or say shit or just get nasty when they're bored or anxious or scared, which pretty much covers every emotion we feel here every hour of every day.

What's strange is how I feel. I'm annoyed, but I'm not out-of-my-mind incensed the way I was in Laredo when that jerk called me the c-word. I'm not even sure what I want to do. I feel numb.

I hear Paul's voice. *Pick your fights.*

I tell Rigsbey to gather our platoon.

"I'm sure some of you know what this is about," I say, pacing in front of my Marines, and then I tell them about the writing on the bathroom wall. I tell them that I find the action rude, disrespectful, inappropriate, and childish. I tell them that I'm upset, but mainly that I'm just tired of this shit. "We have a job to do. We don't have time for distractions. I'm gonna ask you two favors. One, if you know who did it, tell me. I'm gonna assume it wasn't one of you, that it was somebody from another platoon. I really hope that's the case. Second favor. Clean it up. The next time I go in there, I don't want to see it. That's all."

The next time I go in the bathroom, a dirty white smear painted like a crude wide Nike stripe covers up some writing I can't read. *I am so tired of this shit*, I say before I throw up.

So, so tired.

》》》

I really don't know why, but a few days later I go after Rigsbey. We're getting ready for our second convoy in three days, and while we're walking across the base, he starts talking trash about the differences between men and women. Men are superior in most things, he claims. One great example: driving. He points out that because I never learned to drive a stick shift I couldn't drive a bulldozer, and that makes me inferior. And then he gets insulting. I tell him to stop, I'm not in the mood, but he pushes it, keeps railing about horrible women drivers. I again tell him to stop. He just laughs, and then I shove him in the chest.

He looks stunned, then he shoves me back, meaning it. I go for him.

It's stupid, I know, crazy. Rigsbey is freakishly strong and a martial artist.

We grapple. I flip him and pull him down. He rolls away, cuts my legs, and tries to pin me. I catch him across the face with my open hand, slicing his cheek with my fingernails. He howls. Pissed, he works his weight onto me and finally pins me. I tap him, and he lets me up. We're both panting and feeling ridiculous and embarrassed. Thankfully, we're behind the vehicle and equipment shed, and nobody has seen us. I untangle my hair and throw my cap at him. "Your face is bleeding," I say.

You're flipping out, Theresa, I shout to myself.

Am I reaching my breaking point?

❱❱❱

I lose track of time. Each day blurs into the next. I can barely distinguish morning from night. I fight exhaustion. I walk on legs that feel as flimsy as sticks. Sometimes I'm so weak I don't remember walking at all. My body feels detached from my brain. My eating disorder, which I now acknowledge as full-blown bulimia, consumes every moment that I don't distract myself with work. I throw up . . . four times a day . . . five . . . six . . . feels like every other hour. . . .

But I suck it up. I keep my head in the game. I fight through it.

Until I can't.

15

HITTING THE WALL

DECEMBER 14, 2005 / FALLUJAH, IRAQ

I PULL MYSELF UP OFF THE BATHROOM FLOOR. I GRIP the sink and stare at my reflection. My eyes look sunken. I spit into the basin, turn on the faucet, and splash water onto my face. I rinse my mouth. Then, my hands shaking, I reread the last paragraph of my dad's letter.

"The irony of your situation is that you are in a war, *your enemy* is not from without, but from within. . . . You are a very courageous person, Theresa, for facing your problems straight on. You cannot hope to take care of others properly if you cannot take care of yourself . . . ."

I know I have lost.

I have lost my war from within.

>>>

One last convoy. A night mission. The night before the general election.

Tomorrow the Iraqi people will elect 275 members of the newly created Iraqi Council of Representatives, 25 percent of whom, according to new Iraqi law, must be women. I have no particular love for the local Iraqi politicians I've met, and I certainly have issues with the way Iraqi men treat women, but I want to be a part of this historic vote. I feel I have a stake in this. I want to leave my mark in some small way.

We've been assigned to set up seven polling sites and to place jersey barriers and other obstacles around them. If need be, from the moment the polls open until they close, we'll guard voters from attack. Our intelligence reports that turnout will be high.

In addition to leading the engineering platoons, I will work with a logistics platoon, overseeing 150 Marines. I will be running thirty trucks, the largest convoy I've ever run.

"Why do we need all these trucks?" I say to Rigsbey, who now sports a scraggly scar on his left check. "What the hell are we carrying?"

"I don't know. Feels like we got about ten trucks too many."

I know this is no ordinary convoy. During the hours before the mission, my gunny and I attempt to coordinate and corral what feels like a thousand moving parts, organizing and designating combat-ready Marines along with heavy and light equipment, jersey barriers, polling site obstacles, tools, and weaponry into Humvees and a flock of ten-tonners and forty-foot flatbeds. Rigsbey pulls me aside and whispers that the colonel has decided to come along.

"Great, awesome," I say. "What vehicle is he going to be in?"

"I won't get in your way, I promise," the colonel says, appearing behind me, his voice booming, his grin bright as a floodlight. "I just want to come along for the first drop-off."

"You're more than welcome to ride with us, sir," I say.

"We're making history, Lieutenant," he says. "You don't mind if Sergeant Vickrey comes along, do you?"

"The supply Marine?"

"You won't even know he's here."

"More the merrier, sir," I say, not meaning it.

A couple of Marines step aside, and Sergeant Robert Vickrey, a gawky, out-of-shape gear snob, presses his way forward. He wears his freshly pressed, right-out-of-the-box combat gear, including knee pads, elbow pads, shiny high boots, and leather gloves that match his leather pistol carrier. He looks like he's leading a parade.

"You fucking kidding me?" I murmur to Rigsbey.

"John Wayne lives," he murmurs back. "I just figured out why we've got thirty trucks instead of twenty. The other ten are filled with lookie-loos who want to tell their grandkids they were the ones who ran the election."

"Pisses me off," I say loud enough for everyone around to hear, storming off to put out yet another fire.

Yes, we're making history, but this mission is *hot*, right from the start. If ever a convoy were put into the line of enemy fire or found itself rolling down a road laced with potential IEDs, this would be the one. I have never felt more exposed, more on edge, or more responsible for my Marines.

Rigsbey and I head over to the chow hall for dinner, but I can't eat. I don't have any desire for food right now because I will only throw it up. Still, I know we will be out all night, and I will need something to sustain me.

"You really should eat something," Rigsbey says, loading up his plate.

"Too much on my mind right now," I say, stuffing a handful of chocolate and peanut butter energy bars into my pocket.

I imagine eating those energy bars, excusing myself, and throwing up in the middle of the desert behind some puny, scrubby bush.

I nearly gag at the thought. My saliva tastes raw and sour.

Rigsbey gathers my Marines around a fire outside, and I present my five-paragraph order for the mission. For the next fifteen minutes, I offer part orientation, part specifics, and part pep talk. I start slow, speaking softly, then I speak with authority and passion, explaining the details of what we will be doing and where we will be going.

I look at these men, all of them listening with rapt attention. My Marines. I karate-chop the air as I speak, my volume rising, a tick below a scream, and I know . . . this is my last time. I will never again speak to a group of Marines like this. I will never give another five-paragraph order. At least not here, not in Iraq, not for Operation Iraqi Freedom.

Not until I save myself. Not until I set myself free.

》》》

We leave in the rain, right before midnight.

We drive down murky, slippery roads, weave around sinkholes, rumble by craters in the sand, trembling stacks of smashed and twisted metal, mounds of garbage, buildings collapsed into piles of rubble, burned-out shells of cars, corpses of emaciated animals.

A war-torn country, I think. *A future land of the free.* What are we doing? What the hell are we doing?

I feel weak, weaker than I can ever remember. I should have eaten dinner. I should have eaten something.

We arrive at the first location, an open space in the desert bordered by a rickety stack of smoldering ruins, a hill of garbage, a heap of dirt, and a hole in the ground packed with jagged pieces of wood resembling sharks' teeth. A town, formerly. I scramble out of my Humvee and direct a group of Marines to unload and set up a perimeter of jersey barriers around our first polling place. While the Marines work, I check and recheck my map, verifying that we have come to the right place. The work done, the colonel and Sergeant Vickrey wave and veer off in their own Humvee.

We roll out down a main road, arrive at our second polling place, another remnant of a ruined town off a grubby road. Another row of burned-out and collapsed buildings, more hills of garbage, the stench knocking me back as I step out of the Humvee, my stomach growling and then flipping. As I coordinate unloading the jersey barriers around this second makeshift polling place, I feel like I'm walking in a dream. I try to peer ahead, into the dark of the desert, and see nothing—no movement, no life, only a black vastness. Suddenly I feel vulnerable. I step to the side of the lead Humvee and look down the road into this funnel of nothingness.

"We're sitting ducks," I say. "There could be roadside bombs everywhere."

I'm paranoid, I think, and climb back inside the Humvee, the third vehicle in the line of thirty.

I'm suspicious of this road, and I don't trust our map. I study the GPS, and after a moment I identify on the monitor a side road that will take us to our next destination quicker. A shortcut. I inform Tampon, my communications Marine, that I'm calling an audible. We're going to steer the convoy off the road we've mapped out and go for the shortcut shown on the GPS. For a few minutes, chaos rules as I explain through our various lines of communication that we're going slightly rogue, taking this new route, receiving a rather cool "as long as you know what you're doing" vibe from the captain back at COC. Good to go, the convoy veers off onto the shortcut. I suddenly feel light-headed and unsteady. I reach in my pocket for an energy bar, rustle the wrapper, then change my mind and slide my hand out. I close my eyes and try to center myself.

The convoy bumps along for another twenty minutes, and Tampon, his eyes riveted on the GPS monitor, starts waving frantically at the screen, then shouts, "Stop! Hold up! *STOP!*"

The lead truck grinds to a stop, and all the convoys ease up behind. A huge concrete wall blocks the road, closing us in. We've come to a dead end.

"Shit," I say.

"There was no wall on the map or on the GPS," Rigsbey says.

"Fuck," I say. "We have to turn around."

"Why the hell did you stop?" The captain is howling at me from COC through my headset. "Are you *lost?*"

"We hit a dead end," I say.

"Unbelievable," the captain says. "Get those trucks turned around and get back on the main road!"

"Yes, sir."

"Why did you take that shortcut?"

"I thought we would make up some time—"

"You thought. Turn those trucks *around.*"

"We have to back them up, sir. It may put us behind schedule."

"Fuck."

It takes thirty minutes to back up the convoy, wheel all the trucks around and get them facing toward the main road. I'm on the move constantly, communicating with COC, running from vehicle to vehicle in the rain, consulting with Tampon, scanning the GPS monitor, checking the roadmap, trying to tamp down the gnawing feeling that as we turn the trucks around, we're completely naked, open targets for enemy fire. Finally, the convoy re-aligned, I radio in to COC and head out. I check my watch. We're an hour behind schedule. I feel sick.

We roar onto the main road, back on our original route to the next polling place. I pick up binoculars and look on all sides, focusing on the landscape, determined to complete this mission without a further hitch. I shouldn't have improvised, even if taking that shortcut made logical sense. I should have stuck to the plan. But we're back on track, no harm, no foul. We can make up the lost time.

I get a call on my radio.

A hundred feet ahead, our reconnaissance Marine has spotted a large paper bag by the side of the road.

His voice crackles through my headset. "What's your call, ma'am? Do you want the convoy to ride past it or do you want to call in an EOD?"

"Possible IED," I say.

"Yes, ma'am."

I don't hesitate. "Call it in," I say, and turn to Rigsbey. "Hold up the trucks. We have to wait on EOD."

I have never shaken the image of the IED blowing up the Humvee in our sister convoy and killing that corpsman. I picture his face and his smile, and I shiver. I don't care if the captain goes berserk or what anybody else says, we will wait for the bomb squad. I refuse to take the risk.

It takes an hour for EOD to arrive and another half hour for them to determine that the paper bag contains trash and not a bomb. Factoring in going down the dead end, we have now lost more than two hours. I don't care. We may be late, but we're alive.

I give the go signal, we fire up the trucks, and the convey thunders toward our next polling place drop. Almost immediately, the captain's voice blasts through my headset like a knife into my brain. "You just wasted an hour and half sitting on your ass, waiting around for something *that wasn't even a bomb*?"

"That's right, sir," I say, never feeling cooler, more confident, or more in control. I pause, not for effect but because I'm pissed. "It wasn't a bomb, but it could've been."

"But it wasn't—"

"It *could have been*." I drop my voice. "No way am I putting a hundred and fifty Marines in harm's way. I'm not taking that chance, sir."

"Just . . . carry on," the captain says.

The headset clicks to silence.

The rain letting up, we unload jersey barriers and set them up at the remaining five polling sites. Our mission complete, the convey returns to Camp Fallujah at 7:30 A.M., two and a half hours later than our estimated 5 A.M. arrival. I have spent a nightmare night of frenzied and chaotic communications, going from radio to radio, staying in contact with the logistics company, the captain, COC, and the thirty vehicles in the convoy. I feel like I have been juggling chainsaws for eight hours straight.

>>>

The thirty vehicles safely tucked in, my 150 Marines squared away, the elections *on* somewhere out there, the crack of intermittent mortar fire a backbeat, the civilian population protected behind our jersey barriers under the watch of platoons of combat Marines, the now famous purple fingers of those who've voted pointed high, my mission accomplished, I call my dad. As soon as he hears my voice, he cries, and the moment he starts crying, I cry with him. He tells me he has been on his knees praying for me, asking God that I be safe, and now that I am safe, he tells me that he is going to get on his knees and pray that I get well. He begs me to call a doctor he knows at Villanova. I promise him that I will. A sniveling mess, I click off the phone, then I go into the chow hall and binge. I pile a plate with pancakes, eggs, and hash browns, fill a bowl with cereal, wolf it all down, and then go into the bathroom and throw up.

Sickened, dizzy, I return to my room and eat all the energy bars I've accumulated, sprint into the bathroom, and throw up.

I go back for a second breakfast, slam it, throw it up.

I eat a third breakfast and throw up.

I throw up eight times.

Wasted, disgusted, and lost, I crash onto my cot and within seconds, mercifully, conk out, dead to the world, for the rest of the day and into the night.

When I wake up, I use the satellite phone to call the doctor at Villanova. She picks right up, as if she is expecting my call. Through my garbled words and jerky voice, fighting tears, I tell her how sick I feel, how much I throw up, and that I don't know what to do.

"I'm sick," I say. "But I can't leave my Marines. I can't abandon them. I just need to get better. . . ."

I can't speak anymore.

"Theresa, listen to me," the doctor says. "You cannot heal in a combat zone."

I try to open my mouth to respond. I can't. My mouth feels nailed shut.

"Do you hear me?"

I do. But I can only nod.

>>>

The next day I ask Rigsbey to go for a walk. We stroll along the perimeter of the base wearing flak jackets, shouldering our weapons. We've been through hell, the two of us, and I've come to trust Rigsbey with my life. I tell him so. He starts to reply with some smartass remark, his default, but he must sense that something's different about me, something's changed, because he just nods and mumbles, "Me too."

I stop and look away from him, and I say, with no run-up or intro, "There's something wrong with me."

"What do you mean? Are you sick?"

"Yes."

I turn and look him in the eye. "It's my heart," I say. "I think. They think. The doctors." I'm too ashamed to tell him the truth.

He scowls and kicks the dirt. I don't know if he buys the lie.

"Well, get the help you need," he says. "Immediately."

I duck my head and sniff. Rigsbey gently reaches over and lifts my chin. "Seriously," he says. "Don't wait."

"I will," I say. "I am."

"Good," he says.

I don't think he buys the lie.

»»»

That evening I tell the captain the truth.

I find him in his office, alone, sitting at his computer, surfing the web for a football game. I sit down across from him without an invitation, and before I lose my nerve, I blurt, "I'm going to tell you something that I've been holding in for a while. I'm sick. I've been throwing up a lot. Actually, all the time. I'm not sure what to do about it."

He looks pained. "I had a feeling something was wrong. I've been worried about you. You look very pale. Not well."

I bite my lip, surprised at the kindness in his voice. I wonder if I have to explain anything further—that I'm *making* myself throw up—and then he says, "My girlfriend in college had bulimia. I kind of know what you're dealing with."

I start to cry. "I'm not a hundred percent, sir. Especially running all these missions . . ."

I dab my face with my thumb.

"We could decrease your workload," he says. "I can arrange that. Or, if you want, I could send you to another base to do admin work—"

"I just . . . I need to go home," I say.

The words hang there.

"I'm not trying to escape deployment at all, sir, but I'm no good to anyone out here the way I am. It's not fair to the Marines. I'm not able to lead them. Not the way I am."

Neither of us speaks for a long time. I hear voices outside, guys hollering, laughing, trucks roaring, an occasional pop of distant mortar fire, the high-pitched chanting that's become so familiar. Noises of the night.

"Sir," I say. "I have to go home."

>>>

The next morning the captain takes me to see Colonel Quinn, the regimental combat battalion commander. We've worked together four times, pulled four all-nighters. He's expressed support, encouragement, even admiration. I expect he'll understand what I'm going through.

I explain how sick I am. As the tears flow, I tell him that I feel as if I'm in a battle with myself. The colonel leans back in his chair, shoots a glance at the captain, then looks back at me. "What is it that you want from me?"

I'm crying full out now, so I can't really see straight or think straight, but I hear the displeasure in his tone. Disappointment maybe. And then an undercurrent that I identify.

He thinks I'm lying.

He doesn't accuse me of lying to get out of my deployment, but I know that's what he's thinking. I just know it. He might as well scream it. I don't care. I blow past it.

"I need to go home, sir," I say. "I need to get help."

"You don't want to go to another base, take a less stressful job until you get a handle on this?"

"No, sir. I have to go home."

He waves his hand in what looks like dismissal.

"Okay, if that's what you want, you need to talk to the captain of the Fallujah Trauma Center. He'll sign the order. Get you to go home. And that'll be it."

Thank you for your service.

The colonel stands, offers me his hand. He's done with me.

>>>

The last stop.

The Navy captain in charge of the entire medical unit in Fallujah. Med head. Tall, caramel skin, grim-faced, mocha eyes serious and unblinking. I walk into his office, and I can tell he's been *told*. He's waiting for me. First time in Iraq I feel like I'm walking into an ambush.

I don't sit. He doesn't stand. He eye-rolls *me*. Given how many times I've eye-rolled others, I guess I deserve that. But I don't deserve the look of sheer disgust he sends me.

"Sir, I need help."

That's all I get out. Tears rush down my face in torrents. I try to choke them back. I can't stop sobbing. I am in a mental hurt locker.

"You sure this is what you want to do, Lieutenant?"

I nod.

"What? You're going to have to speak up."

"Yes, sir. I'm sure."

I want to say that I thought I could handle my problem, but I couldn't. I didn't respect my eating disorder. I didn't think it was legitimate. I stood by helplessly as my disorder became a disease. Now my disease has become a monster and has taken me out. I want to defend myself to the med head. I want to say that I excelled as a leader, that as a woman in combat I kicked ass the same as any guy, the same as the *best* guy. I want to scream that I loved my team and that I put them first, always, every minute of every day.

I want to say all this, but I don't say any of it. I just stand there and bawl, and through the filmy curtain of my tears, I see this Navy captain, the head of the Fallujah Trauma Center, reach to the corner of his blotter and slide a form down in front of him, a form he has already filled out, and without a word or hesitation, he scrawls his signature. He looks up at me then and says, "Okay, I signed the order. You're done."

16

RETURN

I CALL MY DAD.

He cries and murmurs, "I'm so relieved, Theresa. You're doing the right thing. Thank you."

I talk to my friend Adam Lauritzen, my former staff sergeant, and tell him I'm leaving and why. "The Marine Corps will go on," he says. "Take care of yourself. That's all that matters."

I call Kriste. I call two or three other friends. I call Chase, my boyfriend. They all tell me I'm doing the right thing. I don't cry anymore. I'm cried out. I just feel numb.

The day I leave, I meet with my Marines.

I tell them that I'm sick and that I am going home. I tell them it has been my honor to serve with them. I tell them that I am proud of them and proud of the work we've done together. I speak softly, in a monotone. After I talk to my Marines, I pack my bag, moving so slowly I feel like I'm in a trance. After I pack, I go to the chow hall and eat dinner. Every muscle in my body throbbing, I walk stiffly back to my room and throw up in my trash can. I stagger outside and toss the trash bag into the fire pit. Mesmerized, I stare into the pit and watch the flames flickering, reflecting blue light off my face. I finally head back to my room, take a last look around, pick up my duffel, sling it over my shoulder, and walk outside to meet the Humvee that will drive me to the helicopter pad at the far end of the base, where a Blackhawk will fly me to Baghdad, then to Kuwait. From there I will take a C-130 medevac to Germany, where it will refuel and fly to the States, similar to the route I took seven months ago, but in reverse. I've hit rewind. My life is going backward.

We fly at night.

I sit toward the back of the C-130 next to a shell-shocked soldier who walked into the intelligence office on his base holding a makeshift bomb and tried to blow himself up. The bomb turned out to be a dud, and he now sits handcuffed to his armrests, his eyes bulging, muttering, saying words no one can hear. In front of us, in the center of the plane, rows of seats have been removed and replaced with hospital beds filled with the very sick and the seriously wounded. We are an ER of the air.

I sit immobilized, staring ahead, feeling cauterized. I feel as if I've been shot up with some drug that has drained every iota of energy from my being and left me lifeless. I can't speak, I can't move. I cry, my tears pellets. I slam my eyes shut and try to sleep. I open my eyes a slit and sneak a look at the unhinged, suicidal soldier next to me muttering incoherently, and I think, *I am no longer a warrior.*

》》》

We spend three nights in Germany at an Army medical center, a small metal Christmas tree dotted with a few ornaments in the main lobby, the halls decorated with fraying Christmas decorations and children's drawings. Walking the halls between lab tests and psychological exams, I meet two guys in wheelchairs, one who has been diagnosed with crippling sleep apnea, the other traumatized, dealing with a bullet embedded in his brain. I hang out in their hospital room for hours, looking blankly out the window, the three of us ciphers, none of us really speaking. At one point, the guy with sleep apnea asks me, "What are you here for?"

"Heart condition," I say.

Back in my room, an Army psychologist visits me. He checks my chart, asks me a few questions, plays word association, then asks, "Do you want to commit suicide?" As miserable and useless as I feel, I assure him that I do not. I also assure him that I want to get the hell home as soon as possible.

Finally, we fly to the States, and I take up residence for a few days at Walter Reed Hospital in Washington, DC, where I undergo more tests, both physical and psychological. A day before I will be transported to Anderson Air Force Base Hospital for an overnight stay and then cleared at last to return to California to receive a new assignment and treatment for my eating disorder, my dad and Bob visit me. I sit in the one visitor's chair, absently flipping pages in a book and staring zombielike out the window, when they walk in. My dad halts in the doorway, his eyes filled with tears. I leap out of my chair and throw my arms around him.

I pull away and hug Bob, who says, "It's okay, Theresa. You're dealing with it. It's gonna be all right."

We go to dinner. I pick at my food and ask my dad if he can take time off from his church obligations and come with me to California. I don't tell him how feeble I feel, how humiliated, or that I feel like I'm falling into a hole.

"I can't, Theresa, not now," he says. "I did tell the congregation about your eating disorder. The whole parish is praying for you."

I feel so weak. And I feel exposed.

》》》

Travis Air Force Base. The last leg of my medevac world tour before going back to San Diego.

As I walk into the hospital with several wounded soldiers, I'm greeted by a welcoming committee of military wives, girlfriends, and USO members who cheer us as they hold up placards and signs and hand us paper plates of homemade cookies, cakes, and brownies.

I shake a few hands, politely decline the baked goods, all the while thinking, *Why are they doing this? I don't deserve this.*

That evening, I sit propped up in my hospital bed and wait for Paul. My dad has told him about my eating disorder, and Paul has said he will stop in to see me before I leave for California in the morning. I feel nervous for some reason, probably because I haven't seen Paul in a while, and I never know what to expect. We can be best friends. And we can mix like oil and water.

I look up and see him standing in front of me, his six-foot-five-inch frame filling the doorway. He shoots me a half-assed smile. I swing off the bed, and we hug, stiffly. I step back, run my hand through my hair, and offer him the chair. He ambles over to it and sort of collapses into it, his legs stretched out, his hands clasped in his lap. I sit on the edge of the bed, waiting for him to speak.

Paul looks past me, out the window, avoiding my eyes. Finally, he sits up straight and edges forward in his chair. "What happened to you?" he asks.

"What?"

"What the hell happened to you out there?"

A chill squirms down my spine. I feel the tears starting to come.

Please. I don't want to cry in front of Paul. I can't show him how weak I am.

"I got . . . I'm *sick*, Paul."

"You're sick."

He sounds . . . disgusted.

"I couldn't control my eating disorder. I was throwing up all the time. All the fucking time. I got overwhelmed. And lonely. Unfocused. I couldn't give a hundred percent anymore."

"So basically you chose yourself over your Marines."

He might as well have slapped me across the face.

I don't know what to say, so I repeat, "I couldn't give a hundred percent. I just couldn't seem to—"

"You suck it up. That's what you do. You. Suck. It. *Up*."

"I tried . . ."

"You're a Marine. You had a job to do. You couldn't stay out there a few more months? You couldn't fight through this, what, eating disorder? You let it break you? Why didn't you take care of it?"

I shake my head, praying that he will stop interrogating me, accusing me, hammering me. I pray that he will suddenly understand. I grip myself around my stomach. I feel as if I will choke on my tears.

My brother abruptly stands, considers me on the bed, folded over at my waist, my body shaking. He takes a step toward me. He towers over me. "You let everybody down, Theresa."

I know he doesn't mean that. I know he means, "You let me down, Theresa."

My sobs rack me, whamming in my head so loudly that I don't hear him leave.

⟫⟫⟫

I'm flown to California, and I move back in with my sister-in-law, Lisa, Bob's wife, returning to my old room in her apartment in Poway. I report to my commander at Camp Pendleton, a gruff guy in his late thirties who receives me in his office with what's become the standard question everyone asks: "What happened to you?" He assigns me a desk job, battalion secretary, answering phones, responding to e-mails, and scheduling appointments, a world away from escorting insurgents and running convoys. I feel so rejected and dismissed that at coffee breaks I go into the bathroom and cry, scream, or throw up.

By order, I report to a Marine psychologist. I walk into his office and find a wiry guy in his fifties sitting at his desk, furiously scribbling in a notepad. He gestures toward a chair with his pen, and I sit down. After a while, he grimaces at his notepad and without looking at me, asks, "How are you doing?"

Eye roll. "Great."

"So, bulimia. What are those symptoms?"

"What?"

"What kind of symptoms do you have?"

"I throw up."

He writes on his pad. "What else?"

"What else?"

"Tell me more."

"I throw up . . . *a lot*?"

"Uh-huh."

"Have you ever treated anyone with bulimia?" I ask. "Or am I your first?"

He peers at me over his pad. "Would that be a problem?"

"Kind of," I say. "Because, see, I need help. I don't know what I'm doing. And if you don't know what you're doing . . ."

"Let me ask you a few questions."

"Fine," I say.

He asks about my background, relationships with my brothers, my dad, then inquires into my feelings. He pauses, taps the pen against the notepad.

"Well," he says.

Tap, tap, tap.

For the first time he looks at me, studies me, frowns.

"Theresa," he says.

"Yes?"

"I apologize, but this is not my area of expertise. I don't think I'm qualified to work with you."

Tap, tap, tap.

>>>

I see a Navy psychiatrist next.

Heavy-set guy, bubbly, friendly. He greets me with "So, you have an eating disorder," as if he's saying, "So, you think you can dance."

"I do," I say. "Yes. Bulimia."

"Ah. Well, you seem relatively healthy. You look strong, fit. You just seem . . . *down*. Sad. Weight of the world on your shoulders."

"Yes."

"I'm thinking you need to perk yourself up. Change your mood. You need to feel better about yourself."

"I would, yes."

"I think you should consider getting pregnant."

"I . . . what?"

"Are you married?"

"No."

"Boyfriend?"

"Yes."

He raises a suggestive eyebrow. "Well . . ."

"You think I should get *pregnant*?"

"Don't rule it out."

Have I entered the *Twilight Zone*?

"I'm not sure that having a kid—"

"Bundle of joy," he says. "You lack that."

"A kid?"

"No, joy."

"Listen, I have to get back to work."

"Shall we schedule another session?"

"I'll call you."

I race into the bathroom and throw up, thinking, *At least I got the morning sickness part down.*

⫸

I sit at my desk, answering phone calls and e-mails and working with drop-ins to reschedule PT appointments while I wait to hear when I can report for outpatient therapy to begin dealing with my eating disorder. After a week of hearing nothing, I schedule a meeting with my commander.

"Sir, I really need to start therapy," I say to him in his office. "I need to deal with this thing."

"There's a lot going on in the battalion," he says. "The people who got medevaced from Iraq come first."

I gape at him. "Sir, *I* got medevaced from Iraq."

He turns away from me. "You're just gonna have to wait."

⫸

Another week passes.

I'm into my third week back, and I've had two absurd meetings with two inept shrinks and have heard nothing about getting treatment for my eating disorder. I feel completely dismissed. I need *help*. I refuse to wait another day.

I go directly to the hospital commander himself and take a seat in his outer office across from his secretary. I've decided that I will not leave until I'm set up for treatment. I don't care how long it takes. I'll sleep here if I have to.

I explain everything to the secretary. She listens, occasionally jotting something on a pad. When I finish, she says, "Bottom line, you're a combat-medevaced Marine officer, and you have not received your consult for outpatient care."

"Yes. That's right."

"How long has it been?"

"Going on three weeks."

"That's inexcusable. We'll get right back to you. I promise."

She calls me the next day. I have been cleared to attend any outpatient clinic within a reasonable distance of my home for twelve weeks. I thank her, hang up, and schedule treatment at a facility I'll call Hidden Pines, only a few miles from Lisa's apartment.

The battalion commander—my boss—fumes.

"You cut to the head of the line. You can't do that. There's a protocol."

"I'm sorry, sir—"

"How dare you go over my head! Do you know how long my wife has been waiting to be treated for her . . . procedure? Months. You have to wait your turn."

Your wife is not a medevaced Marine officer.

I don't say this. I bite my tongue. And then, my nerves shot, I start to cry.

"You think you're so special," he says.

"I don't," I say. "I'm not."

"Damn right you're not. You're just selfish."

>>>

My replacement in Iraq arrives at my desk one morning. He looks agitated. "I'm deploying," he says. "Taking over for you."

"Oh, okay, well, if you have any questions, or if there's anything you need—"

"No, I'm good." He rocks back and forth, fiddles with the pens I keep in a coffee cup on my desk. "Too bad you didn't make it through deployment."

I smile thinly.

Finally, someone who's sensitive to the fact that I'm sick.

"This is pretty fucked," he says.

"For sure," I say, assuming he means my disease, but suddenly I wonder if I'm misreading him, and I ask, "What is?"

"My deployment. My wife is furious."

"At me?"

"Damn right. I have to go over there and clean up your mess."

The room goes as frigid as a meat locker.

"I didn't leave because I wanted to—"

"No," he says, not listening to me, not caring anything about me. "I don't need anything from you. Why would I? You couldn't make it through deployment. You got nothing for me."

>>>

I go for treatment at Hidden Pines, eight hours a day, three days a week. The other women there—they are all women—suffer from bulimia and anorexia. I relate to their symptoms and their living with the anguish and secrecy of their diseases. I don't relate much to *them*. None have served in the military. And it may be my imagination or insecurity, but I sense that most of them consider me strange, an outsider. To them, I appear fit and strong and healthy.

Most of these women have been living with their eating disorders for years. Some have spent a decade in and out of institutions and outpatient clinics. They don't seem to be making much progress.

That will not be me, I tell myself. I'm here to get better. I need to get better.

In group, we talk, we share, we listen, we hug, and we cry—oh, how we cry. But I can't shake the thought that these women seem resigned, even defeated, as if their disease is their destiny.

It's not their fault. In some sense, they believe their eating disorder is their husband, son, daughter, best friend. Their eating disorder is the love of their life.

Of course, they're wrong. Their eating disorder is a fiend disguised as the love of their life. Their eating disorder is the devil.

While I don't get much out of group, I enjoy art therapy, where I sketch drawings that help me explore my fixation on my body and body image in general. I also start journaling again, ferociously, filling notebook after notebook, my anger and fears bleeding out on the pages and expressing the sadness and pain I feel over leaving the Marines and my strained relationship with Paul, my sentences smeared with tears.

The idea to journal this intensely comes from my behavioral therapist, Dr. K, a kind, calm young woman I see twice a week. Dr. K seems to "get" me, identifying me, correctly, as a doer—someone who thrives on having tasks to complete, missions to accomplish, no matter how small. She sees me as who I am: a Marine. Dr. K offers me practical tips, little rules, which I incorporate into my life—never eat in the car; always eat sitting down; create specific times to eat during the day; never use the word *"fat"*; be kind to myself; don't put myself down; and if I feel the urge to binge and purge, call someone on my list of five people, whose names and numbers I've written down in my journal.

I start to look forward to my days at Hidden Pines, especially to my sessions with Dr. K. Soon I notice that I'm throwing up less often. I don't consciously decide to throw up less often; I just stop. Then, while writing in my journal one night, I realize something that surprises me: I want to succeed—I want to cut down the times I throw up—not for me, but for Dr. K. I wonder then if that's how I live my life. Do I live to please everybody else—my boyfriend, brothers, teachers, superior officers, and, especially, my dad? Is that me, someone who never tries to please herself?

Dr. K and I start to make progress, teeny steps. She encourages me to do something, anything, just for me. And then my insurance runs out, and my time at Hidden Pines comes to an end.

17

EXIT STRATEGY

2006 / CALIFORNIA

I HATE MYSELF. I FEEL SO LETHARGIC AND FAT. *Damn.* I'm not supposed to use that word. But as I jog around the high school track at dawn with my sister-in-law, Lisa, I feel more out of shape and uncomfortable than at any time in my life. Lumbering like an elephant, my running shoes crunching the red clay, I ask myself, *Why did I agree to train for a freaking triathlon?*

I list the reasons: I need to get in shape; I suck at swimming, and this will be a good excuse to improve that; the triathlon will be held in Hawaii, one of my favorite spots on earth; I love Lisa, and this is an opportunity to work out together and hang out, just the two of us; I'll be part of a team—I thrive when I'm on a team—and I want our team to be among the leaders in raising money to fight leukemia and lymphoma, the theme of the triathlon; and the number-one reason—I have a vague belief that by training hard, getting in shape, improving my swimming, hanging out with Lisa, raising money for a good cause, and going to Hawaii, I will stop throwing up and feeling like shit.

I hate that I'm not the best runner, best triathlete, best performer on our team. I know that some of our team members are in recovery from leukemia, but somehow that information doesn't dent my twisted thinking. When it comes to physical performance, I need to be the best. Period. I'm always the best. That's who I am, bulimic or not.

The absurdity of all of this doesn't sink in until one night, when, suddenly feeling a desperate urge to scream for no reason and then puke my guts out, I call Kriste, number two on my call list after my dad, and nod dumbly at the phone as she talks me out of shoving my face into a moist lemon pound cake that rests teasingly in front of me on the kitchen counter and then sprinting into the bathroom and barfing. Listening to myself prattle on, I realize how ridiculous I sound, how distorted my thinking has become. I remember Dr. K and several others during group at Hidden Pines repeating endlessly, "Your eating disorder will mess with your mind. It flips simple logic upside down."

Somehow during the call with Kriste, I manage to turn logic right side up. The people on my team are the superstars, not me. They're running, biking, and swimming despite having had fucking *cancer*. They are the top performers by far. I'm not competing with them; I'm supporting them. It's not a cool thing to do, it's an honor. I train with them and I feel inspired.

For the triathlon, Chase comes with me to Kona and cheers on the whole team. I have mixed feelings about spending this time with him. I'm not sure how I feel about him. I'm not sure how I feel about anything. But I'm certainly having second thoughts about continuing our relationship. I put those on the back burner as I carbo-load the night before the triathlon, then throw up—I really didn't want to, but shit, I ate so much. I wake up at six, and Chase drives Lisa and me to the starting line.

I actually do okay in the triathlon. I even make it through the swimming portion without getting eaten by a shark, a stressor and a concern. I meet our team at the finish line, all of us jumping around, embracing, crying, and posing for photographs. I'm not real excited about that last part because my mind tells me that I'm overweight and I look like crap, but at the awards ceremony afterward, I receive a certificate for raising the most money of anyone who entered the event.

At least I won something.

That kind of twisted thinking poisons my every waking thought.

>>>

I sit at the conference table across from the JAG officer. Everything in this lawyerly room looks shiny, new, and polished—the floor, the walls, the conference table, even the JAG officer himself. His hands folded in front of him, his face nondescript, his eyes cold, we discuss my exit strategy from the Marine Corps.

Well, *he* discusses my exit strategy. I listen and nod. For months now, since returning from Iraq, I have not felt like much of a Marine, at least not the Marine I trained to be. I want to shout at this guy that I am not a secretary or a receptionist. I am an officer, a leader. I am a warrior.

At least I was. I sit at my desk every morning, my legs jumpy, often cramping from inactivity, my nerves jiggling, my eyes bleary, my head listing forward or to one side, threatening to drop onto my blotter as I fall asleep.

To be honest, I want out of the military. I have come to the end. I know I will not be sent back into battle. I know that in the best-case scenario, I will remain behind that desk, running out the clock. I need to speed up my departure. I need to cut myself loose as soon as possible. I have to get out.

The JAG officer presents two options. I could seek a medical discharge, but someone has written that my eating disorder indicates a personality disorder. Because of that a medical discharge is not guaranteed and will take time. Or I can go for an administrative discharge under medical conditions.

The voice I hear—my voice—sounds robotic. "What's quicker?"

He shifts in his chair and speaks as if reading from a manual. "I have to explain that administrative is usually under dishonorable, but we can give you administrative honorable with a medical condition. We would have to check one of four categories that explain the discharge. Standard procedure. Best we can do with administrative honorable would be to indicate substandard performance. That's the best we can do. That's what I would recommend. We can expedite your administrative discharge—your honorable discharge—in approximately one month."

"What about a medical discharge? How long would that take?"

"Six months."

"*Six months?*"

"Minimum. Could take longer. I've seen it. And again, no guarantee."

I feel my throat seize, my head swim. "You're gonna give me honorable? With administrative?"

"Yes."

"Administrative doesn't look as good, though. We both know that. I do have a medical situation. Which I'm dealing with." I shake my head slowly. I feel trapped. "Six months?"

He shrugs.

"The only box you can check on the form is substandard performance? That's not true."

"I'm giving you your best choices. My hands are tied."

"I can't wait six months. I'll go insane. I have to get on with my life."

"Administrative honorable. That's your best option. In my opinion."

I don't know why I don't argue more. I don't know why I accept this. I don't know why I allow this "substandard performance" designation to follow me, to taint my record. The disease has worn me down, upending my logic. My sense of survival pushes me to move forward as fast as I can. I feel defeated. I'm too exhausted and too beaten down to fight anymore. I make my choice.

I reach over and sign my honorable administrative discharge agreement.

It's over.

I receive my preseparation checklist in the mail. I follow all the instructions carefully. I take my required final physical and dental exam. I fill out and sign sheaves of paperwork. I clean and tidy up my gear and return everything. I hand in my weapon. I sit for my exit interview. I say a few goodbyes at the base. I walk through all of this in a haze, as if I'm drugged.

My last day at Camp Pendleton I feel relief. Nothing else. I want to feel more. I wish I felt more. But I don't. I'm desperate to move on. I remember my mother's words: *Move forward. Don't look back. Life must go on.*

>>>

I leave Lisa's place and move up the coast to a small beach house in Redondo Beach. I have no real direction, just some vague notion of wanting to work in athletics or sports training, having rejected my previous notions of becoming a firefighter or a cop. Through a friend, I meet a sports performance coach and trainer at Velocity Fitness who encourages me to become a personal trainer and pays me minimum wage to shadow him.

At Velocity I meet another intern, Lauren, a woman my age, formerly a top-ranked college tennis player. Lauren and I become instant friends, meeting for coffee regularly, playing beach volleyball after work and on weekends, partying hard with a group of volleyball players, and ultimately sharing tales of boyfriends and eating issues. Lauren, it turns out, also suffers from an eating disorder.

For a fleeting moment I consider a career in nutrition, dismiss that, and decide to apply to physical therapy school. At the same time, I'm making a few dollars on the side as a private pitching coach.

One day I get a call from a former teammate on the Brakettes. She's heard that I've left the service and has a proposition for me. The Nouro softball team in Sardinia, a professional team in the Italian League, needs a pitcher, and she has recommended me. All I need to do is contact them, send a video, and she's certain Nouro will hire me.

"I haven't pitched in four years. I'm totally out of shape."

"That won't matter at all," she says. "They stink."

I check them out online. She's right. They stink. I send them a video. They offer me a job.

I call my dad and tell him I'm going to Italy to play professional softball. He can't hide his disappointment. "You're not going to school?"

"I'll go when I get back."

"Sounds like you already made your decision."

We both go silent, each waiting for the other to speak.

"I guess it's a good opportunity," he says, begrudgingly.

"Thanks, Dad," I say, trying not to sound sarcastic.

Chase flat-out hates that I'm heading off to Italy. "What about me?" he asks over the phone, his voice whirring into a whine.

"What about you?"

"Fine. What about us?"

"Chase, I care about you, but this is something I want to do."

"So your mind is pretty made up."

"It's totally made up. I'm going. I'm gonna play softball in Italy."

"All right then." He exhales theatrically. "See you . . . sometime."

I train with Lauren, running the beach every morning and working out after hours at Velocity. As my departure day for Italy approaches, nerves grip my stomach. I've always loved going on new adventures, but if I'm completely honest, in this case I just want to get away—from making a commitment to Chase, from pleasing my dad, from trying to figure out my life. I want to escape.

18

THE ITALIAN JOB

2007 / SARDINIA, ITALY

W E PRACTICE DURING THE WEEK, PLAY ONE GAME
on the weekend, occasionally two. We play our home
games in a tiny stadium with an all-dirt infield, the
outfield mostly weeds.

Sardinia being an island, we travel to road games in a prop
plane, playing in equally cruddy stadiums. We draw sparse crowds,
home or away, but we do attract our regulars, mostly creepy, horny
local guys or enthusiastic lesbians. Our coaches are two fiery
Cuban guys who scream at us nonstop in either blisteringly fast
Spanish or mangled Italian, not a word of which I understand. To
ward off the infamous Italian gawkers who descend on me whenever I walk the streets and to announce to our stunningly challenged fielders that a batted or thrown ball is headed their way, I
learn one essential Italian word: *occhio*, meaning "look out!"

We go bowling after every game. I find this ritual off-putting, especially when we lose, which is practically all the time. We're professionals, paid not only to play but to win. As the team's main pitcher and, well, as me, I cannot stand to lose. I sulk, I bitch, I replay each pitch in my head, I blame my teammates, but most of all, I blame myself . . . for not striking out every opposing batter, for not making my team better, for *losing*. And then, although I try not to, although I'm writing in my journal, meditating occasionally, obsessing less over what I eat—having abandoned Fit Forever *forever*—I throw up.

I hit my lowest point after we lose a tough road game. I sit steaming and silent on the plane ride back to Sardinia, a short hop of less than an hour. I feel unusually annoyed when we get back home, and as usual, the girls head out to the bowling alley.

"You're seriously going *bowling* after a loss like that?" I ask my catcher.

"Why not? The game's over. Life, however, is not over. You have to move on."

I go to the bowling alley, but I don't bowl. I drink what feels like an entire pitcher of cheap Italian wine and binge on Italian bar food, then I make three trips to the bathroom to throw up, the most I've purged since I checked into Hidden Pines. I go home that night and scribble pages and pages of gibberish into my journal, tear the pages out, ball them up and toss them into the trash, and throw up again. I wake up feeling hungover and disgusted and sick. My hands shaking, I call the catcher and ask her to meet me for coffee.

"You look terrible," she says, sitting across from me at a table in a corner of the coffee shop.

I tell her about my eating disorder. I'm not sure why I do it—

maybe because I've always felt close to my catchers—but I feel that I have to. I tell her about leaving Iraq and how I've been dealing with my eating struggles through outpatient therapy. When I finish telling her, I feel as if I've purged.

"If there's anything I can do," she says, "any way I can support you, let me know."

I thank her, then I say, "I *hate* to lose. I feel so shitty, and because I feel that way, that gives me permission to throw up. I feel awful, but it's not enough. I want to feel really awful. Does that make sense?"

She takes a moment. "You're taking it too personally. You didn't lose. The team did."

I take this in, then I say, "How do you do it? How are you not upset when we lose?"

"I am upset. I'm very competitive. But I did my best. I left everything on the field."

The catcher leans in. "Theresa, most things are out of your control. You certainly can't control whether you win or lose. You can only control how hard you work and how hard you try."

An hour after she leaves, I remain seated at the table, staring into my empty espresso cup, the worst moments of the last year unspooling in my mind.

"I was a great Marine," I say. "I left because I was sick." *You can't control being sick. Most things are out of your control.*

>>>

We lose the next game.

I blindly crash around the bowling alley, knock over a chair, gorge, binge, eat too much, go into the bathroom, and throw up. Then I go home and throw up again.

I wake up in the morning feeling hungover and horrible. I sit in a chair, press my knees against my chest, and say the catcher's words aloud: "Most things are out of your control."

I suddenly feel something new. For the first time since I've been struggling, I feel . . . anger. Rage. I am furious at my eating disorder. I scream at it. *Why are you doing this to me? Why can't you leave me alone? Why can't you get out of my life?* Then I say, "That's it. I don't care if we win or lose. From now on, all I care about is getting better. Doing the best I can."

We lose the next game.

We meet at the bowling alley. I bowl a few frames, suck, and then I sit down with the catcher and some other girls, and we all order food. I binge. I eat enough for two people. Then I go home and . . . *I don't throw up.*

The next morning I feel hungover and bloated and disgusting, but I don't throw up. I go for a run. After that, I go to the gym, where the cute guy who works the front desk gives me a high-octane smile. I smile back.

After my workout, we have practice. In the dugout, preparing to jog out to the mound, I look out at the brown dirt carpet of an infield and feel my hands trembling slightly. Behind me, as she finishes snapping on her shin guards, the catcher says, "Are you all right?"

"No." I narrow my eyes, hoping I won't cry. "But I will be."

That night we all go to dinner at a local café, and again I eat too much. I go home and I don't throw up. "Fuck, I'm uncomfortable," I say. "But, okay, I'm just gonna have to be uncomfortable. That's the way it's gonna be. Maybe if you eat a little less at night, you won't feel this shitty." I look longingly toward the bathroom. I don't move. I don't throw up. I feel awful, but I don't throw up.

A week goes by, then two. I eat too much most nights, and I feel like crap when I get home, but I don't throw up. I run in the mornings, work out afterward, try my best at practice and during games, but it doesn't matter; we don't do well, losing more often than we win. Gradually, I start to eat less at night, and I feel less uncomfortable. And I don't throw up.

I go to a coffee shop one day. I open my journal, start writing, and realize that I have to purge. I have to purge the toxins from my life. Chase. I start with him.

He hasn't been all bad—he has been kind and supportive—but he has also been controlling. And while I consider him to be my first real love, I've clung to him for all the wrong reasons. The relationship represents my disease. I need to let it go. I need to let him go. It will require courage, and I will seek help in a few weeks when I return to the States. But I will purge Chase.

I also must purge my reliance on my dad. I love him, but I need to let go of anything that controls me. I need to move on without fear, allowing myself to stumble, fall, feel confused, feel uncertain, even screw up, because—I write this in big block letters—I'M NOT PERFECT. I'm not the perfect sister. I'm not the perfect girlfriend. I'm the not perfect pitcher. I'm not the perfect Marine. I'm not the perfect fitness pageant contestant, friend, roommate. I'm not the perfect daughter. I don't have to be. I don't want to be. I just want to *be*.

Jolted by the screech of the espresso machine, I raise my eyes from my journal and realize . . . I was perfect at one thing. I was a perfect bulimic. Not anymore.

I flip to the back of my journal and write two words that fill an entire page.

I'm done.

I put down my pen and stare across the coffee shop. I feel lighter, as if someone has lifted a crushing weight off my chest. For the first time in years, I can breathe.

I.

Am.

Done.

19

RECOVERY

AND SO, IRONICALLY, MY RECOVERY FROM MY eating disorder begins in a coffee shop in Italy, a country the world associates with food.

I begin by literally turning the page. I turn to a blank page in my journal and write, "May 11, 2007. Day 1." I jot down a few thoughts, but I know my words don't matter. What matters is I have given up my emotional commitment to softball, and I will begin a new game. The game of my life. Each day will be an inning. Each hour a pitch.

I make three promises to myself. I will give up control. I will abandon being perfect. I will love myself. The way I am. I know the game will never end. My journal is my scorecard.

Day 2. "One day down, good. I feel lighter. Clearer. Less hungover."

Day 3. "Two days down, good. I feel like crap."

I'm like an alcoholic. Every alcoholic knows exactly how many days she is sober. I'm Theresa. I'm a food drunk. I am two days sober.

Day 4. "Three days down, good. I'm beautiful. I say that because I feel like shit. I want to throw up. I will not."

Some days are hell. Those days I summon my mother. I think about her gentleness and grace, but I evoke her fighting spirit. I imagine the pain she felt and remember how she suffered, and still she fought. These days I allow myself to suffer. I allow myself to feel uncomfortable. I tell myself to believe in my body. I learn to trust that the feeling of discomfort will pass. I know that slowly my body is finding its normal state.

Keep going forward, Theresa. Don't look back. Keep moving.

I tick off one more day . . . and another . . . and another . . .

Two weeks down, good.

Three weeks down, good.

One month down. Good.

I never throw up again.

>>>

I stay with Chase in Yuma, Arizona. I try to talk to him about our relationship, expressing my doubts, concerns, and the overall feeling that we just don't fit. I try to make him see what is so clear to me: we rely on each other, but we're not right for each other. All of the psychobabble I've heard and associate with us rages in me, most commonly the terms *enabling* and *codependent*. He either doesn't understand or refuses to understand what I'm talking about. He smiles wanly during my impassioned attempts at conversation and shrugs off my lingering feelings of doubt. Frustrated, I write him a letter, which I insist he read in front of me so we can discuss it afterward. He reads the letter and says he doesn't get it. He wants to talk marriage, and I want to talk breakup; we're that far apart. Doing all I can not to sob, I tell him that I love him, but I'm saying goodbye. As I walk out of his apartment, blinking in the blinding afternoon Arizona sun, I feel light-headed, unmoored, and . . . relieved.

I crash temporarily on a friend's couch in Los Angeles, lugging my two seabags stuffed with all of my earthly possessions, having no place to live but envisioning the direction in which to steer my life. After breaking my toe in Sardinia, I searched in vain, first in Italy and then in the States, to find a physical therapist who could help me with the healing process. During that pursuit, my career path revealed itself to me: *I* want to be that person. I want to be a physical therapist. All pretentiousness aside, I want to be a healer.

I enroll in a couple of classes and look for a place to live in Long Beach, a suburb of LA. I'm determined to find an apartment by myself, but my dad insists on coming out from Pennsylvania to help me move. For the first time since I can remember, maybe the first time ever, I resent my dad coming to my rescue. I don't want his help. I don't want him treating me like a little kid. As we trek from apartment to apartment, my dad shooting down every one— "This one's too small, this one's so dark, this neighborhood's not safe"—my anxiety comes to a boil. It's all I can do to keep myself from screaming.

"You're starting school in a week," my dad says. "You didn't plan this very well, Theresa."

"I'll find a place, Dad. I'll figure it out."

I want to tell him, *Dad, please don't criticize me, and please don't preach to me. Just be my dad.*

I see a therapist. I address head-on why I became so sick. I ask myself the hard questions: why do I push myself so relentlessly in everything I do? Why do I feel I have to live my life pleasing everybody else, especially my brothers and my dad? Why am I so obsessed with being the best? Why do I feel the need to control everything? Will I allow myself to give up everything in my life that controls me?

I journal, I meditate, I question choices I made, and I start to see a new way to live. I embrace the idea of moderation and begin to abandon my need to live in the extreme. I discover some life-changing epiphanies: *Theresa, you're a grown woman. You don't have to share every single thing with your dad anymore. You can keep some things to yourself.*

My relationship with him shifts. We talk often but not every day. I share my life with him, but not every moment, not every detail. This shift feels right. It takes time, but we slowly evolve from daddy and daddy's little girl to father and daughter.

>>>

I move into a small one-bedroom in an apartment complex that feels like a little community—pizza parlor and coffee shop on the first floor, people my age all around, volleyball games and barbecues on the beach. I start training for my second triathlon, and while going for a run, I bump into a neighbor, a fellow workout nut. We run that day, start training together on occasion, and become friends. We text each other regularly, I bring him soup when he comes down with a cold, and I often drop in unannounced for a drink, none of which goes over big with his soon-to-be-ex-girlfriend.

My neighbor starts badgering me to meet his new roommate, a guy he's sure I'll like. I tell him thanks, but I'm off men and dating for the foreseeable future.

"This guy's different," he says. "You like football players, don't you? He used to be our quarterback."

I file away the information and put off meeting the roommate. One day I pop in to see my neighbor after playing beach volleyball with my new friend, Jennifer, a woman I've come to adore.

"Can't stay," I tell my neighbor. "I'm on my way to jujitsu class."

"I thought you were this martial arts guru. You learning anything there?"

"A rear naked choke," I say. "So this is how you choke a guy." I grab him from behind and slap a chokehold on him.

At that moment, the roommate, Per, walks in. He's tall, handsome, confident, but very preppy. Not my type. After I remove my hands from his roommate's throat, he introduces himself.

"Per?" I say. "Like the fruit?" He smiles shyly. "You must've heard that, what, a thousand times?" I ask.

I invite him to a barbecue and volleyball game with my extended beach "family" the next day. He shows up with a bottle of wine—very thoughtful and classy—and fits in with everybody. I notice that he's very comfortable with my friends and doesn't need me to entertain him. I also notice that I can't keep my eyes off him. After everyone leaves, he asks me to go salsa dancing with him. So not my thing. Plus, honestly, we're a mismatch. He's prim and proper and kind of looks like a banker. And I'm this . . . farm girl. But somehow I find myself at this cantina salsa dancing, laughing, and losing myself in his smile and . . . could it be I'm falling in love?

Later, after we've become a couple, I ask him when he knew we were meant to be. Per says I had him at "So this is how you choke a guy."

Shortly after Per and I start dating, I find out that I have been accepted into PT school fulltime in the fall, which will eventually direct me toward graduate school and becoming a doctor of physical therapy, a journey that will take several years. Even as Per and I get serious, I plan a four-month trip around the world. My friends, Jennifer among them, ask me, "What about the boyfriend?"

"I care about him a lot, but I'm doing this trip. If he's not willing to stick it out with me, then forget it."

Per not only supports my going on a four-month worldwide adventure, but he arranges to join me for part of it.

I start in Hawaii. I go to Fiji and New Zealand for a couple of weeks. I meet up with friends from the Marines and head over to Melbourne, where I crash with the shortstop from the Italian softball team. I run and hike, drive the Great Ocean Road, smash up a rental car, encounter a koala bear, fly to Sydney, and rendezvous with Per. Our relationship heating up, we spend a week in Australia snorkeling in the Great Barrier Reef, a highlight. We hop over to Thailand and experience the Full Moon Party at Koh Phangan—thirty thousand people dancing feverishly to techno music on a white sandy beach beneath the brightest full moon on the planet, the entire spectacle reminding me of how much a partier I am not. Per and I stay in Thailand for another week, and then he goes back to the States and I continue to Switzerland, then Spain, where I meet up with Kriste, my dear friend and college catcher. I go on to France and Amsterdam, and finally London, missing Per on this second leg of the trip more than I ever imagined I could miss anyone.

>>>

One day toward the end of my physical therapy program, I find my niche.

Working out at a crowded CrossFit gym in San Diego, I notice several "wounded warriors"—veterans also called adaptive athletes—one living with traumatic brain injuries, the others amputees. I find myself drawn to one particular athlete, a double amputee, a burly guy who has had both legs cut off above the knees. A trainer works with him, giving him cursory instruction on how to accomplish a dead lift, lifting a bar from the floor to his waist. The trainer seems distracted. He looks past the athlete, then leaves him standing over the bar as he heads off to work with someone else. The adaptive athlete exhales, grabs the bar, wobbles on his artificial legs, drops the bar, nearly loses his balance, and then slowly steadies himself.

From my spot twenty feet away, I meet his eyes.

He stares at me and then turns away. He dangles his arms, considering the bar at his feet.

My legs begin to carry me toward him. I want to help him. I don't have a specific plan—I'm not an official trainer yet—but I have an idea. But as I walk toward him, I feel nervous. *Will he accept me?* I think.

I reach him and extend my hand. "How's it going? I'm Theresa. What branch of service were you in?"

"Marines. I'm Gus," he says, shaking my hand.

"Nice to meet you." I look at the bar. "How much weight you got there?"

"One forty-five."

"Awesome." I nod. "Hey, I hope you don't mind, but I had a thought. I noticed you had trouble with balance. Plus I saw that your back got very rounded. You need to protect it. If you leaned against the wall and slowly lowered the bar starting at the top, it would help your balance."

"I'll try it," Gus says.

I carry the bar to the wall, Gus following. I turn and face him. "If you keep your spine in a neutral position . . ." I gently touch his back. I freeze. I stare at my hand.

I used to put those fingers down my throat. My fingers were tools of abuse. Now I rest them on Gus's back. I'm using them as tools for healing. I keep staring at my hands, my fingers splayed along Gus's spine.

"You all right?"

I look at him. "Yeah," I say. "I'm fine. I just . . . I'm sorry." I slowly bring my hand to my side.

"Been through some stuff?" Gus ask.

"Yes."

"I know the feeling."

We both smile.

I spot Gus. He has enormous upper-body strength and even more willpower. He blasts through three sets of dead lifts. When he finishes, he swipes his forehead with a towel. "Thank you for helping me, Theresa."

"Anytime." I pause. "The hardest thing is asking for help, isn't it?"

Gus lowers his eyes. I cannot express how much I feel connected to him. He looks up. "People ignore me. They look the other way." He swallows. "Sometimes I think I'm invisible."

I reach over to him and again allow my fingers to touch his shoulder. He touches my hand and simply nods.

I know then that I've found my calling. I want to work with wounded warriors like Gus. He and other adaptive athletes show their wounds to the world. They have no choice. But I too have wounds.

You just can't see mine.

In the summer of 2009, after I've endured a long period of no communication, my brother Paul calls me. He talks vaguely, mentioning the ups and downs of his business.

He's reaching out, I realize, as I pace in my apartment, offering a sympathetic ear.

He pauses and says, "I wanted to tell you . . ." The phone goes silent. He clears his throat. He speaks very softly. "I've talked to Bob and I've talked to Dad. I just want to say, Theresa, that I'm . . . proud of you. For making such a major change in your life. And getting through everything the way you did. That took a lot of courage. I'm *very* proud of you. So, yeah, that's really all I can say."

It's so much, I want to tell him. No. It's everything.

⟫⟫

Over Christmas, Paul comes down from Sacramento, settles on my couch, and stays with me for a couple of weeks. I show him where I work out. We drive to Hollywood and watch the filming of one of our favorite TV shows, *CSI: Los Angeles*. I introduce him to Per, and they hit it off, as I knew they would. And I introduce him to my good friend Jennifer. They *really* hit off, as I also knew they would. In a surprisingly short time, my good friend Jennifer becomes my sister-in-law.

On April 13, 2013, Per and I marry in front of a close circle of friends and family at Mission San Miguel, a historical landmark built in 1797, on California's central coast. My dad says mass and gives me away to the groom. Heather, my dear friend from my first two years at Villanova, does my makeup. Jennifer, my sister-in-law, fixes my hair. To honor my mom, Kriste, my maid of honor, and I buy my wedding dress for $300 at Brides Against Breast Cancer, a nonprofit. We hold the reception at Mondo Vineyards in Paso Robles. We honeymoon in Costa Rica and Panama. Per is definitely cutting it.

20

WE'RE ALL REALLY TRYING

"The secret of strength lies in a quiet mind."
— WHITE EAGLE

I START EACH DAY BY GIVING MYSELF A GIFT: ONE hour first thing in the morning. No distractions. No phone. No computer. I sit outside with a cup of coffee. I love the morning light. I raise my face toward the sun.

I go inside then and meditate for thirty minutes. I clear my mind. I remove the clutter that rattles inside my head. I focus on my breath. I slow myself way down. I try to quiet my mind completely.

I eat breakfast. I sit at the table or the counter, and I eat slowly. I enjoy what I eat. Yes, I enjoy food.

After I eat, I step into the bathroom. I wash my face slowly. I take my time. The bathroom remains my safe place. I still sometimes escape here. But instead of purging, I breathe. I seek out calm and quiet.

It has taken me six years to get to this place.

I have not thrown up in all that time.

I have discovered how important it is to cleanse, to try to remove the toxins from your life. They eat away at you. They mean to destroy you. It is a daily battle.

I have learned to embrace vulnerability. To do that, I have to reach deep within myself. I find an inner strength more powerful than I could have imagined. I summon a reservoir of strength, resolve, and courage to fight my enemies within. The fight comes when I fall. I win the fight when I get back up. And when I push forward. I live my mother's words.

We all face wars inside us. Our foes are self-doubt, regret, loneliness, loss, fear of failure, and the need to be in control. Our weapons are love, good friends, exercise, healthy eating, rest, and living in each and every moment.

I have realized my calling. I am a doctor of physical therapy running my own practice, which combines strength, conditioning, and movement medicine. As part of my practice, I teach a CrossFit class called "Adaptive Strength" for wounded warriors, helping them develop strength, redevelop body balance, and improve their mobility. I am the instructor, but these men and women teach me much more than I could ever teach them. I work with a mother of two—a former Marine—who wages her war with adrenal cancer. I work with a young veteran who lost his leg above the knee in Afghanistan. I work with a double amputee who served in Iraq. I work with a Navy officer who was sexually assaulted by one of her peers.

They share their stories, they reveal their vulnerabilities, they give me their hearts. We laugh, all of us, and we cry sometimes.

They curse, not at their plight but at not being able to do one more rep or push themselves for thirty more seconds. "*Yet*," I tell them. "You haven't done that one more rep *yet*." We work together; we cheer each other on. This is my new team, the team I lead, the team I pitch for now.

I also try to help people find their quiet mind. I help them seek inner peace. And I tell them to ask for help when they feel lost or afraid. I tell them that asking for help makes you strong.

Asking for help makes you a warrior.

I am a warrior.

EPILOGUE

IN SEPTEMBER 2014, MY DAD, JOSEPH HORNICK, signed up for a grueling hundred-mile bike race, riding in the name of one of his parishioners who was dying of cancer. Because of previous commitments at his church, my dad could not participate in the official race, so he decided to ride the hundred-mile route himself, on his own time, the weekend before.

At the eighty-mile mark, in a remote area of Pennsylvania, my dad suffered a heart attack and fell off the bike, onto the road. He died an hour later.

In his too-short life, my dad helped save many lives, including my own. As long as I am alive, his spirit will never die.

I dedicate *Warrior* to him.

Acknowledgments

THERESA

Gratitude for my Love: Per Larson—my amazing husband who is my partner for life, adventure buddy, and someone who is patient, kind, and whom I am excited to spend my life with.

Gratitude for my family: For your love and unconditional support. I am thankful I was finally able to listen not only to myself, but to open up to all of you. Thank you for your love, specifically Paul for doing your best to love and support me during my struggle. I always have and always will look up to you. To Bob—for being the voice of reason and someone who always keeps it real. Thank you for helping me understand that my decisions were courageous. To Lisa—thank you for letting me be your roomie, triathlon buddy, and loving sister in law. To Jennifer Hornick—first for being my close friend, and second for being the best wife for my big brother Paul. You have amazing strength. To my ninja niece and nephews—Leora Morgan, Adam Lars, and

Ryan Joseph, and to Jenny Larson for your beautiful heart in opening up to me and being the big sister I have always wanted. To Katya, Adam, baby Talia, and Avery Mosowicz; my in-laws Charles and Adrianna; Noelle, Casey, and Tanya—for your love and unconditional support. To Trevor—for your openness in sharing your warrior story. To Joseph, Maryssa, Daniel, Aiko, Hillary, Matt, Duke and Millie McNerthney, Shannon and Brent Hall, Michael Ross and his late wife Molly, Dutchess and Larry Maddock, Patrick and Paige McNerthney, Jane Lintner and Matt Von Boecklin, Uncle Dennis, Aunt Lee, Mike, Theresa, Mikey, Brittany Hornick, and my Grandmother Mary Hornick, who is 100 years young.

To my late mother Mary Ann Hornick, who taught me how to live in my short time with her, for her words, her love, her time. To my late Dad—for being the best Dad he could be and my biggest fan. Thank you for giving me a heads-up about the reality of life, people, experiences, and helping me become the woman I am today.

Gratitude for my coauthor: Alan Eisenstock, I am thankful you were in attendance at the 2013 NEDA Conference where I first truly opened up about my story. You believed in me and the power of my story because it was the story of many, and you helped me use the platform of this powerful book to have a voice. I also very much appreciate your friendship through this process of writing key stories in my life that are funny and also painful, through losing my father, and through the ups and downs of life these past couple years. You have been there. Thank you!

Gratitude for my literary agent: Anthony Mattero, thank you for believing in my story. Thank you for your persistence in helping me understand how impactful a memoir can be and sticking up for me in the publishing world.

Gratitude for my social media rep: Daffnee Cohen, for being a shining bright light in the online world that can be so daunting.

Gratitude for my publishing dream team from HarperOne: Hilary Lawson, I feel like we could be sisters if the W in your last name was an R. I am so thankful for your energy, support, and tremendous and thorough editing skills. You helped me overcome a lot of fear about getting my story out there. Thank you for your "go for it" spirit and "I have nothing to lose" attitude. Thank you for believing this story will affect and be relatable to millions. To Suzanne Wickham—my publicist who was so fun to work with and create media game plans with. Her energy is boundless as well as her persistence and diligence with getting me the exposure I needed to make this book create waves was amazing. To Kim Dayman—thank you for your thorough marketing help. I appreciate your time, your attention, and the diligence you showed with helping me grow my brand so that people will better understand my message. To Noël Chrisman—for not missing a beat on helping make this book more polished.

Gratitude for my friends: Kriste Romano—my best friend and sister for life, whom I can always, always, always count on. I am blessed to have you in my inner circle and really do not know what I would do without you. Kelly Gaida (Acuna)—for being a bright light in college and beyond. I admire your resilience and am grateful for your friendship. You are my sister from another mother. Casey McDonald—thank you for consistently reminding me that asking for help was a sign of courage, not weakness. I needed that reminder often, and sometimes still do. Katie Hollier (Chou)—for your friendship, support, and sanity check while serving in the Marines and as civilians. To Adam Lauritzen, Father John Endres, Jim Cahill, Heather Milner, Joanne Romano, Rick Romano, Kate Hendricks Thomas, Kelly and Juliet Starrett, Randall Martin, Troy Willis, Christa Schinelli, Grant Foreman, Sarah and Jim Hodge, Brett and Ben, K. J. McManus, Alec Zirkenbach, Cogen and Sara Nelson, Michael Hernandez, Nico Marcolongo, R. T. Davis, Maggie Hannon, Ashley Hope Linder, Josh Klein, Maria Dibernardi, Linda Goss, Karen Newinski, Megan O'Leary, Jackie Pasquerella, Mia House, John Stratton, Shelly Gwynn, Leslie Malerich, my Villanova softball team, the Brakettes softball team, my Italian softball team, the Adaptive Strength CrossFit class, Charlotte Brock, Anneke Marvin, Carly Lemler, Jill Miller, Joanne Whitney, Ret. Colonel Paul Pugh, Hilary Achauer, Chef Wallace, Sara Olson, Max Conserva, Christian Little, Garrick, Sarah Taylor, Maria Kang, Timothy Hall, Scott Rigsbey, all the Marines in 2nd platoon at 7th Engineer Support Batallion, Seattle Prep High School, Jeff Pietz, Bill Busey, Susie Stark-Christianson, Becky Clinton (Pebble), Anders Varner, Bryan Boorstein, Justin Fields, Neil Patrick, T. J. Murphy, Clint and Kim Russel, Claudia Chaloner, Annemarie Alf, Megan Hersh, Ray Regno, Dianna DiToro, Marcus Krauss, Erik Larson, Hunter McIntyre, Ryan Krupa, Alex Delacampa, Alessandra Wall, Leon Chang, Charlotte Hickingbottom, Jason Anderson, Ray and Megan Fernandez, Candace Coles, Capt. Stafford, Rad and Maureen Ferland, Stephanie Superka, Jacquie Hawes, Mary Ellen Salzano, Eva Selhub, Kim Dennis, Karen Leyva, Ellen Lowe, Ed Kane,

George Bryant, Paul Krumenaker, Kevin Justice, Chuck Hayes, Kionte Storey, James Richard Kao, Ty Sommerlin, Joleyne Boyle, Ed Paulter, Donnie Fricks, Andy Nava, Jodie Peyton, Deborah Kull, Kristen Garcia, Joe Desena, Jimmy Moore, Bryan Sargent, Robert Scribner, Leah Brown, Chappie Hunter, Jessica Law, Christopher Browning, Jerry Hall, the late Joe Cuffaro, and Juan, Veronica, baby Tony, and Rosario Barrera.

Gratitude to organizations: Movement Rx, MobilityWOD, National Eating Disorders Association, CrossRoads Adaptive Athlete Alliance, CrossFit, Challenged Athletes Foundation, Operation Rebound, Resiliency Project, Linder Kids, Fathom Cross-Fit, Horse of the Sun, Team Red White & Blue, and lululemon athletica.

To anyone I may have missed, my apologies!

To all my Warriors out there:

Yeah you! You are not alone, and what makes you a warrior is that you show up! You show up, you want to be engaged in your life, you ask for help if you need it, you do the best you can with what you have, and you treat others how you want to be treated. Your wounds—visible and invisible—do not go unseen, and they also do not define you. My mission for you is to get quiet daily, surround yourself with quality people, and allow yourself to live the most authentic, genuine, unfiltered life you can. What do you have to lose? Nothing! You better believe I enter the arena of life daily ready to go and it does *not* always work out in my favor, but I keep fighting, as should you . . . warrior!

ALAN

First, to Theresa. Thank you for your courage, commitment, patience, and passion. Thank you for making Warrior your mission. Thank you for trusting me.

To everyone at the National Eating Disorders Association and, especially, in memory of Lynn Grefe. Thanks to you, I met Theresa. Thanks to you, the world is a healthier place.

To Anthony Mattero, superstar. Period.

To everyone at HarperOne: Nancy Hancock who found us, and Team Warrior: Mark Tauber, Suzanne Wickham, Noël Chrisman, Alison Petersen, and, in particular, Hilary Lawson, eagle-eyed leader of the pack and master literary surgeon. It didn't hurt a bit.

To the home team: David Ritz, my literary lifeline; Madeline and Phil Schwarzman, Susan Pomerantz and George Weinberger; Susan Baskin and Richard Gerwitz; Kathy Montgomery and Jeff Chester; the Barrabees—Loretta, Lorraine, Linda, and Diane; Alan and Ben; Chris and Nate; Ed Feinstein; Gary Meisel; Linda Nussbaum; Randy Turtle; Jay Eisenstock; and Jim Eisenstock, WWII warrior, war hero, and my hero.

To the greatest family on earth: Bobbie, Jonah, Kiva—and now Randy—and Snickers the Wonder Dog, and in memory of Z and GG.

Finally, to anyone who struggles with an eating disorder or with disordered eating of any kind, I wish you strength, clarity, and recovery.

About the Authors

THERESA LARSON has been a semiprofessional softball player, an award-winning fitness competition contestant, and a lieutenant in the Marines, where she led an entire platoon while deployed in Iraq. She is now a doctor of physical therapy and the founder of Movement Rx, offering support to wounded warriors and individuals with movement issues. Theresa travels all over the world as a speaker for the CrossFit Movement and Mobility course and is a consultant for the world-renowned MobilityWOD. She is a Lululemon ambassador and works with Team Red White & Blue, LinderKids, the Resilience Project, the National Eating Disorders Association, and other nonprofits. She lives in San Diego, California.

ALAN EISENSTOCK is the author of fourteen books, including *Raiders!*, *In Stiches* with Dr. Anthony Youn, *Cancer on $5 a Day* with Robert Schimmel, and *The Kindergarten Wars*. He lives in Pacific Palisades, California.